Eating

and

Drinking

with

God

Alliance of Confessing Evangelicals 600 Eden Road
Lancaster, PA 17601 AllianceNet.org

The Scripture references used throughout, unless
otherwise indicated, are from the Holy Bible English
Standard Version (ESV), Classic Reference Edition,
copyright 2001, by Crossway Bibles, Wheaton, Illinois.

ISBN: 978-0-9980102-2-9

Eating

and

Drinking

with

God

Ken Golden

ALLIANCE
OF CONFESSING EVANGELICALS

Contents

Foreword

If you pick up one of the traditional Reformed
confessions or catechisms and read its statements on
the Lord's Supper, you'll find a clear, succinct, and
robust view of what this sacrament is. You wouldn't
get any impression that Reformed Christians have any
issue with the Lord's Supper.

And yet, if we're honest, we must admit that many
Reformed Christians *do* have something of a problem
with it. Let's say that their relationship with the Lord's
Supper is a bit awkward. They know that their churches
ought to celebrate the Supper and that they ought to
participate, because Scripture says they should; but they
don't understand exactly why it's important, or what
blessing they'll miss if they fail to partake.

The awkwardness I have in mind doesn't stem from
lingering suspicions about Roman Catholicism. It's
true, of course, that one of the Reformation's chief
concerns about Rome was its understanding of
transubstantiation and Eucharistic sacrifice. Early
Reformed theologians recognized that the Lord's
Supper could be abused, and this concern has
remained in the back of Reformed Christians' minds
until the present. But many other biblical doctrines and
practices have been abused as well, without therefore

becoming awkward for the Reformed. Awkwardness toward the Supper must concern something more than a reaction against Roman Catholic teaching.

Perhaps this awkwardness stems from the differences between the Supper and Scripture. One of the great achievements of the Reformation was its elevation of the reading and preaching of the word as the primary "means of grace." The Reformers recognized the sacraments as genuine means by which Christ bestows grace to his people, but taught that the word was the primary means and the sacraments secondary. The Holy Spirit works through the word to *create* faith, while the Spirit works through the sacraments to *confirm* faith. The word can be effective even without sacraments, while sacraments do not even exist apart from the ministry of the word. This primacy of the word meant that Reformed churches put sermons at the center of every worship service and encouraged ordinary believers to study the word individually and with their families. These practices have been formative for Reformed Christianity, and I believe we can be very grateful for that.

Yet word-centric-ness may lead some to question the other means of grace. This is especially true if we assume that the sacraments are supposed to work in the same way the word does. When we read a biblical text or hear a sermon, we can often describe rather easily how it profited us. We can explain what we learned from it. We can ask our children on the way home from church what the sermon was about. We can identify what sin in our lives the sermon exposed, or what encouragement the sermon provided.

But things don't work in the same way with the Supper.

We can't explain what we learned when we ate the bread and drank of the cup on a particular Sunday morning. We can't identify what particular sin the Supper exposed, or what particular encouragement it offered. We can't ask our children what the Supper was about that morning—at least not in the way we ask them about the sermon. And if we can't explain what we learned or how we were challenged by the Supper... then what? Are we just supposed to *feel* something, or *experience* something? Should we feel more holy, or more comforted, or more heavenly-minded? Speaking from personal experience, I often have people approach me after I preach and tell me with appreciation that they'd never before seen something I mentioned in the text, or had never thought about that text in the way I presented it. But I don't think anybody has ever told me, after I've administered the Supper, that they'd never experienced eating the bread in the way they just had. It's no coincidence that some Reformed churches offer opportunity for sermon discussion with the pastor after worship services, but none that I know of advertise a Lord's Supper discussion.

The Covid-19 pandemic provides an interesting occasion for reflecting on these matters. During these times, it seems that most Reformed Christians have continued to listen to their pastors minister the word to them in some remote format or another. To be sure, watching one's pastor speaking from an empty sanctuary or in his office is not the same thing as a sermon preached to the gathered congregation. Yet we can still describe what we learned, discuss it with our children, identify exposed sins, *etc.* Yet during this time we have not been able to celebrate the Lord's Supper—

and many Christians, I suspect, would not consider this such a great loss. They may know theologically *that* they've missed something, but have a much harder time understanding *what* they missed, and how this lack has been spiritually detrimental.

Ken Golden is here to help. In his previous books, Pastor Golden has proven himself adept at explaining important things in a concise and simple way, and this new work is no different. He has thought and taught about the Lord's Supper a great deal in his time as a minister, and he now presents the fruits of his reflections to a broader audience.

This little book, in its own way, should help many believers get over their awkwardness around the Lord's table. Golden shows the biblical requirement for the Supper, but he also explains why Reformed churches administer it in the way they do, what's going on when Christians partake in faith, how it serves as a rich Spiritual blessing in Christ, and why we ought to celebrate it frequently. If you want straightforward assistance in understanding and appreciating the Lord's Supper, this work was written for you. I trust that as you study this little volume, you will come to desire the Supper more, miss it more earnestly when it's not available, and long more zealously to participate in the wedding supper of the Lamb, to which our present Supper humbly points.

David VanDrunen
Westminster Seminary California
September 2020

Before We Begin

The love of food and drink is universal. Around the world, people express this love affair through acts ordinary and extraordinary. Some share recipes, while others safeguard the cuisine of their heritage. Some live to satisfy their cravings. There's some truth to the saying that the way to a man's heart is through his stomach!

Food and drink make life worth living—gluttony and drunkenness excluded (Prov. 23:21). The love of food and drink is itself a gift of God. According to the sage Qoheleth,

> There is nothing better for a person than that he should eat and drink and find enjoyment in his toil. This also, I saw, is from the hand of God, for apart from Him who can eat or who can have enjoyment? (Eccl. 2:24-25).

While there are many culinary options, some things never go out of style. Among these universal staples, bread and wine share pride of place. From crusty artisan loaves to pre-sliced sandwich stackers, there's a bread for everyone. From dry Barolo to robust Chianti to sweet Moscato, there's a wine for all tastes. According to well-known Spanish proverb, "With bread and wine you can walk your road."

Yet bread and wine aren't only physical gifts from God; the Lord also combines them with spiritual blessings. He incorporates them into the sacrament of the Lord's Supper, a spiritual meal He shares with his people. Through bread and wine, God's people enjoy intimate communion with their Savior Jesus Christ and grow in His grace.

This book embraces the Lord's Supper as a spiritual meal. Before you even open the book, the cover invites you to a celebration, an opportunity for eating and drinking with God. Each chapter unpacks this invitation: from explaining the nature of the spiritual meal to the different "flavors" (*i.e.* ways) of understanding it. The book answers various questions, such as:

> *Who can attend?*
> *How often should it be served?*
> *What food and drink should be used?*
> *Who should be serving?*
> *How us this connected to our future destination?*

In discussing these themes, my primary goal is to cultivate a desire for the sacrament, a longing to eat and drink with God. A secondary goal is to encourage charitable dialogue between people with different views of the sacrament

There are many people who helped make this book a reality. I'm indebted to Justin Alspach, Phil Hodson, Ken Honken, Mark Jenkins, Shane Lems, Christopher Neuendorf, Michael Matossian, and David VanDrunen who read versions of the manuscript and offered valuable feedback. I'm also appreciative of Ben Ciavolella of the Alliance of Confessing Evangelicals for editing the manuscript.

Chapter One

Soul Food and Spiritual Drink

Humans are complex creatures, consisting of body and soul. God formed us out of the dust of the ground (Gen. 2:7a). He gave us bodies, making us physical creatures, and nourishes our bodies with physical things. The Lord provides food to satisfy our hunger and drink to quench our thirst.

But that's only one aspect of the person. God also breathed into us the breath of life (Gen. 2:7b). He gave us souls, making us spiritual creatures. So if He provides physical things for our bodies, how does He nourish our souls?

For many Christians, the answer is obvious: God nourishes our souls with His *word*. In the Old Testament, listening to the Bible was equated with eating and drinking (Isa. 55:1-2). Jesus also spoke this way in his earthly ministry. As he was tempted in the wilderness, he quoted an ancient truth: "Man shall not live by bread alone, but by every word that comes from the mouth of God" (Mt.4:4, *cf.* Deut. 8:3). Clearly, the Bible is food for the soul, drink for the spirit.

Yet God offers a full course meal for his people. Besides the word, the sacrament of the Lord's Supper also nourishes our souls. At the Last Supper, Jesus instituted His sacrament in a most unforgettable way. It's told in three gospels (Mt.26:26-29, Mk. 14:22-25, Lk. 22:14-20) and mentioned in one epistle (1 Cor. 11:23-26). All four accounts speak of a connection between sensory things (bread and wine) and spiritual realities (Christ's body and blood). They share the provocative statements: "this is by body" and "this is my blood of the covenant." Luke and 1 Corinthians also include the language "new covenant in my blood" and the command "Do this in remembrance of me."

These words have led people to different conclusions. Some view the sacrament as a mere symbol pointing back to Christ's words and historical actions. Others see something deeper. Rather than a bare remembrance, they argue for a real presence; they regard the Supper as soul food and spiritual drink. This chapter supports this deeper, spiritual notion by analyzing some key Biblical texts: Melchizedek's ceremony (Gen. 14:18-20), the Passover and Last Supper rituals (Ex. 12; Mt.26; Mk. 14; Lk. 22), the manna/bread of life discourse (Ex. 16; Jn. 6), and the contrasting spiritual and demonic tables (1 Cor. 10).

Melchizedek's Ceremony

In Genesis 14:18-20, we're introduced to the mysterious figure of Melchizedek. We know he was an important person by his titles: King of Salem and Priest of God Most High.[1] Melchizedek came out to meet Abraham after the patriarch's victory over the eastern kings, and he didn't come empty-handed. He brought a blessing from God Most High (vv. 19-20), the same God that

---

[1] Salem was an earlier name for Jerusalem (Ps. 76:2).

Abraham worshiped. And along with blessing, he brought bread and wine (v. 18). The text even links these things. The blessing (the word of God Most High) was accompanied by the meal (the sacrament of God Most High).

Moreover, the blessing and meal administered by a priest-king of God Most High indicates *divine participation*. One could even say that Abraham was eating and drinking with God. Rather than a banquet for a victorious servant, this was a worship service led by a priest-king. Abraham was receiving God's blessing through the bread and the wine.

Such a mysterious character, this Melchizedek! As the Old Testament unfolds, he fades into the background., and yet he's anything but trivial. Melchizedek the priest-king ends up foreshadowing a greater priest-king, Jesus Christ. Hebrews 7 explains this connection. First, Melchizedek remains a priest "forever", because he has no traceable genealogy (vv. 2-3). Thus, he foreshadows the priest-king who has always existed forever (v. 17, cf. Ps. 110:4). Second, Melchizedek blessed Abraham through word and meal. In a similar way, Jesus blessed His disciples with his words in the context of a meal. In the Lord's Supper, He continues to bless His people (Abraham's descendants by faith) through word and sacrament.

The Passover and Last Supper Rituals

Bread and wine are prominent in the Melchizedek story, but they're best known for their connection to the Passover ritual recorded in Exodus 12. Each household needed to sacrifice an unblemished lamb (v. 5), roast the meat (v. 8), eat in haste (v. 11), and mark the entrances of their homes with the blood (v. 7). The meal celebrated their deliverance from bondage, the blood covering them from God's wrath upon the Egyptian households. This Passover was to be a lasting ordinance after the Israelites gained their freedom (v. 14).

While the Passover lamb was the main course, it wasn't the only food served. Chapter 12 also mentions *unleavened bread*, representing the swiftness of God's deliverance. The exodus wouldn't allow time for any leavening (v. 39). Moreover, this part of the meal was so important that the festival accompanying the Passover would be called by its name. It would become the Feast of Unleavened Bread.

Yet the bread was only part of the equation; the meal also included wine. While Exodus 12 doesn't mention any wine, Jesus assumed its inclusion, and used it during the most famous Passover of all: the Last Supper.

The Last Supper narratives present the Passover in broad brushstrokes. The gospel writers made no mention of the lamb, but focused entirely on the bread and wine. Even though Jesus was the fulfillment of the Passover lamb who takes away the sin of the world (1 Cor. 5:7; Jn. 1:29; Rev. 5:6), he associated his sacrifice with bread and wine.

Let's begin with the bread. The disciples were devout Jews who celebrated the Passover their entire lives. Imagine the shock of seeing their master hold the bread and proclaim, "This is my body." It must have been astonishing. He took the unleavened bread of a practiced liturgy fixed in Israel's consciousness and solemnly proclaimed its fulfillment.[2]

---

[2] D. A. Carson, "Matthew," in *Expositor's Bible Commentary*, vol. 8 (Grand Rapids: Zondervan, 1984), 535.

Redemptive history was etched even deeper when Jesus lifted the cup and connected it with the new covenant in His blood. While it was a departure from the Passover liturgy, His statement wasn't without precedent. Wine was sometimes associated with blood in the Old Testament (*cf.* Gen. 49:11; Deut. 32:14; Isa. 63:3, 6). Of these texts, Genesis 49:11 was specifically concerned with the Messianic seed from the offspring of Judah, who "washed his garments in wine, and his vesture in the blood of grapes."

But the word "blood" shouldn't be separated from the phrase in which it appears. The Old Testament writers commonly associated blood with *covenant making*. Exodus 24:1-8 serves as a case in point. In ratifying the Sinai Covenant, the blood of countless sacrifices was shed on the altar and sprinkled on the people, symbolizing forgiveness and oath-binding.[3] Immediately following the ritual, the leaders of Israel ascended the mountain and partook of a meal. Verse 9 says, "They beheld God, and ate and drank." Details aren't given, but the connection between blood sacrifice and divine communion is unmistakable.

Yet Christ's words instituting the Lord's Supper didn't renew the old covenant for God's people. The fact that Jesus identified the cup as "my blood of the covenant" reveals that He was conscious of His impending death. This death would inaugurate a new covenant with His people—and He would use the wine as a means of connecting His people with the new covenant.

---

[3] Brevard S. Childs, *The Book of Exodus: A Critical, Theological Commentary* (repr.; Louisville: the Westminster Press, 1976), 505-6.

The Manna/Bread of Life Discourse

After the exodus from Egypt, Israel had good reason to be grateful. Yet as they made their way through the wilderness, God's people proved to have short memories. They grumbled about the lack of food and drink, and they even desired to return to Egypt!

Nevertheless, God was patient. He provided *manna*, bread from heaven. The story is told in Exodus chapter 16: Despite their rebellious desire for Egyptian bread, God gave them bread that was both flavorful (v. 31) and plenty (vv. 17-18). He used the manna to test Israel, to see if His people would keep His law (v. 4). Even though they didn't (vv. 20, 27), God continued to provide manna until they entered the Promised Land (v. 35). While it satisfied their physical hunger, something greater would be needed for their spiritual hunger.

The fulfillment would come in John chapter 6. The feeding of the five thousand had just taken place (vv. 1-13), but the crowd misunderstood the miracle. Their bellies were full, but their souls were still famished! This greater hunger could only be satisfied by the fulfillment of the bread: Communion with Jesus Christ.[4] In the conversation that followed, Jesus referred to Himself as the true manna who gives life to the world (vv. 31-35). When they asked for this bread, he replied, "I am the bread of life; whoever comes to me shall not hunger, and whoever believes in me shall

---

[4] The miraculous feedings of the manna, the 100, the 5000, and the 4000 (Ex. 16:15; 2 Kgs. 4:42-45; Mk. 8:1-9) all found their fulfillment in Christ.

never thirst" (v. 35).[5] This caused them to grumble like the original generation that received the manna! And then the imagery took a radical turn:

> Truly, truly, I say to you, unless you eat the flesh of the Son of Man and drink his blood, you have no life in you. Whoever feeds on my flesh and drinks my blood has eternal life, and I will raise him up on the last day. For my flesh is true food and my blood is true drink. Whoever feeds on my flesh and drinks my blood abides in me, and I in him (vv. 53-56).

His hearers were scandalized by these words. They thought he was talking about cannibalism! Moreover, the Old Testament prohibited the eating or drinking of blood because it represented the life of the creature (Lev. 17:14; Deut. 12:23). So how are we supposed to understand this saying?

There are two answers to this question, one primary and the other secondary. The primary answer comes by comparing vv. 40 and 54. In doing so, we discover similar language:

> For this is the will of my Father, that everyone who looks on the Son and believes in him *should have eternal life, and I will raise him up on the last day* (v. 40, emphasis mine).

> Whoever feeds on my flesh and drinks my blood *has eternal life, and I will raise him up on the last day* (v. 54, emphasis mine).

The primary answer is that feeding comes through *believing*. Jesus' opponents didn't believe His words, so they couldn't feed upon His flesh and drink His blood.

---

[5] C. K. Barrett, *The Gospel according to St John: an Introduction with Commentary and Notes on the Greek Text* (repr., London: S. P. C. K., 1975), 236: "The eternal Bread of Life not only created and distributed the food we need, but embodied it as well."

But that doesn't exhaust the meaning of His words. Jesus also mentioned his body and blood in the Last Supper. The sacrament requires faith, but it also requires chewing and swallowing. So even though we eat and drink Christ by believing, we also eat and drink Christ by *partaking*. That's the secondary answer to this question.

Spiritual and Demonic Tables

Some would question the need for extra feeding. "If faith is enough," they would say, "why do we need the sacrament?" The answer is found in 1 Corinthians 10:1-16. Here, the Apostle Paul contrasted two types of food and drink: Spiritual and demonic. The first contrast came from the Old Testament. Verses 3-4 refer to the manna (cf. Ex. 16:13-15) and the water from the rock (cf. Ex. 17:1-7) as "spiritual food" and "spiritual drink." In this context, spiritual meant "of the Holy Spirit" rather than non-physical. The manna and water did satisfy physical needs, but they also had greater goal, a spiritual purpose: God used this food and drink to nurture a dependence upon Him!

Regrettably, the wilderness generation resisted God's purpose. They craved a different kind of food and drink, and became malnourished on idolatry (v. 7). Here, the apostle had something specific in mind: The infamous golden calf episode. He cited Exodus 32:6— "the people sat down to eat and drink and rose to play"—which described the feasting that went along with the idol worship.[6] Rather than causing the people

---

[6] John J. Davis, *Moses and the Gods of Egypt: Studies in the Book of Exodus* (Grand Rapids: Baker, 1971), 285.

to become closer to God, this food and drink drove them further way.

Paul then applied this contrast to his day. As he did with the Israelites of old, the apostle connected the idolatry of the Corinthian culture with eating and drinking. "You cannot drink the cup of the Lord and the cup of demons. You cannot partake of the table of the Lord and the table of demons." Paul didn't mince words. He connected idolatry with a table of *demons*—creatures who cause spiritual harm! And he contrasted this table of demons with the table of the Lord.

What's he referring to? Certainly not the manna and the water from the rock. Those were for the old Israel in her wilderness sojourn. This table is for the "Israel of God" (Gal. 6:16)—the Church of Jesus Christ—as she perseveres in the wilderness of this world. The table, then, which Paul was referring to is the sacrament of the Lord's Supper.

In describing this table, the apostle posed two rhetorical questions:

> The cup of blessing that we bless, is it not a participation in the blood of Christ? The bread that we break, is it not a participation in the body of Christ? (1 Cor. 10:16).

The answers, of course, are yes! The word translated "participation" is *koinonia* which elsewhere means "fellowship", "sharing", or "communion." This is the language of an active relationship. The bread is really communion with the body of Christ; the cup is truly communion with the blood of Christ.

Melchizedek's ceremony, the Passover/Last Supper rituals, the manna/bread of life discourse, and the contrasting spiritual/demonic tables all share a common theme: They show a connection between physical food and a spiritual reality. In doing so, they find their ultimate expression in the sacrament of the Lord's Supper, a meal that offers soul food and spiritual drink for the people of God.

Chapter Two

Theological Flavors

I've just described the Lord's Supper as soul food and spiritual drink for God's people. This means the sacrament is much more than a symbolic rite; it is a spiritual participation in the body and blood of Jesus Christ (1 Cor. 10:16). But this raises more questions. In what way is Christ present in the sacrament? By what means is the bread His body and the wine His blood? And how should we understand the *sacramental union*, the connection of the signs to the reality behind them?

Christians holding to a view of "real presence" have historically reached different conclusions, resulting in divisions in the Church of Jesus Christ. The present chapter considers the "theological flavors" of this debate: Roman Catholic transubstantiation, Lutheran consubstantiation, and Reformed spiritual presence. In surveying these views, a case will be made for preserving the mystery of sacramental union, something the Reformed flavor does best.

Transubstantiation: The Roman Catholic Dogma

The Roman Catholic Church teaches the miracle of *transubstantiation* (lit. "across [or over] the substance") in which the signs become the reality.[1] In Christ's words of institution, Roman Catholics believe "this" and "is" ("*this is* my body, *this is* my blood") describe a metaphysical transformation; what was once bread and wine has permanently become the body and blood of Jesus Christ.[2]

Roman Catholics claim historical support from the early church, yet the first mature formulation dates to the ninth century writings of Paschasius Radbertus.[3] His view, however, was not accepted by everyone. It was opposed by Ratramnus in the ninth century and Berengar in the eleventh century, both of whom defended Augustine's spiritual view dating back to the fourth century.[4] Even so, transubstantiation won the

---

[1] *Catechism of the Catholic Church with Modifications from the Editio Typica*, 1375 (New York: Image, Doubleday, 1995), 384: "It is by the conversion of the bread and wine into Christ's body and blood that Christ becomes present in the sacrament."

[2] The Eastern Orthodox tradition sometimes uses the word transubstantiation, but seeks to preserve the mystery by avoiding discussion of the mechanics. See Timothy Ware, *The Orthodox Church* (repr.; London: Penguin, 1993), 283: "But while Orthodoxy has always insisted on the *reality* of the change, it has never attempted to explain the *manner* of the change."

[3] Philip Schaff, *History of the Christian Church* (8 vols.; 3d ed. rev.; repr.; Grand Rapids: Eerdmans, 1976), 4:547. *cf. Catholic Catechism*, 384-386, which quotes John Chrysostom, Ambrose, and Cyril of Jerusalem as early proponents. See also Herman Bavinck, *Reformed Dogmatics* (4 vols.; ed. John Bolt, trans. John Vriend, Grand Rapids: Baker, 2008), 4:550-51: "From the beginning in the Christian church, it was established truth that the bread and wine were the body and blood of Christ, but the manner in which the union of the two was conceived is not clear and therefore open to various interpretations. This is true of Ignatius, Justin, Irenaeus, and many other writers."

[4] Schaff, *History*, 4:549-550; 564-567; 3:498-99.

day and became Roman Catholic dogma at the Fourth Lateran Council (1215).[5]

Many Protestants have criticized the Roman Catholic dogma as unbiblical and idolatrous. For the sake of ongoing dialogue, this chapter takes a different approach, beginning with some positive statements. Roman Catholics do in fact appeal to Scripture. They find support in John 6:56: "Whoever feeds on my flesh and drinks my blood abides in me, and I in him." This is the language of union with Christ. For that reason, a view teaching a change in substance from sign (bread, wine) to reality (body, blood) could strengthen that union.[6] Roman Catholics also claim their view offers the most straightforward interpretation of Jesus' words. This claim is debatable, but it does promote an objective understanding of the sacrament. Parishioners have little doubt they're receiving the body and blood of Jesus Christ.

The Roman Catholic dogma also has some weaknesses. First, transubstantiation is at odds with Christ's words of institution. Our Lord didn't say, "This is *becoming* my body"; He said, "This *is*." Second, their view doesn't

---

[5] Ibid., 4:568.

[6] *Catholic Catechism*, 1391, 389. Cf. Lawrence Feingold, *The Eucharist: Mystery of Presence, Sacrifice, and Communion* (Steubenville, OH: Emmaus Academic, 2018), 5: "When food and drink are taken into our bodies, they are converted into the very substance of our bodies to strengthen and conserve it. Thus an intimate union is created between the food and ourselves: it becomes one with us. This union is another aspect of the sacramental sign of the Eucharist, for the Eucharist is a sacrament of communion: it creates an intimate union between us and Christ, whom we receive. However, Christ does not become transformed into us, as our food is; rather, the Eucharist transforms us spiritually into a closer image of Christ."

adequately explain the ongoing sensory qualities of the bread and wine. If the signs become the reality, then why do they continue to resemble the signs? Why do the bread and wine still look, smell, and taste like bread and wine?

Roman Catholics have sought to answer this question by locating the "substance" of Christ's body and blood under the "species" of bread and wine.[7] By distinguishing between essential nature and outward characteristics, their theologians could defend the change in substance without requiring a change in how we experience the substance.[8] But there are some problems with this concept. References to the Lord Supper that follow the Last Supper accounts continue to use words describing earthly food and drink. Paul writes,

> The *bread* that we break, is it not a participation in the body of Christ? Because there is one *bread*, we who are many are one body, for we all partake of the one *bread* (1 Cor. 10:16b-17, emphasis added).

Why would Paul call it "bread" when it's allegedly no longer bread, but Christ's transubstantiated body? This would contradict the plain meaning of the apostle's words.[9] Moreover, the concept of transubstantiation results in the spiritual overwhelming the physical. Continuing to exhibit their physical qualities, the bread

---

[7] *The Canons and Decrees of the Council of Trent*, session XIII, chapter III in Philip Schaff, *Creeds of Christendom*, 3 vols., (repr.; Grand Rapids: Baker, 1998), 3:129-30.

[8] Keith Mathison, Given For You: Reclaiming Calvin's Doctrine of the Lord's Supper (Phillipsburg, NJ: P&R, 2002), 240.

[9] I'm indebted to David VanDrunen for this insight.

and wine turn into a sensory mirage. The signs become incidental at best, irrelevant at worst. Such a view compromises the mystery.

Third, and most serious, transubstantiation leads to the worship of the transformed signs. If the bread and wine are transformed, what should happen to the leftovers? They can't be thrown out. They must be consumed, for they're no longer bread and wine but the body and blood of Christ. And if not consumed, what then? Then they must be *worshiped*. The adoration of the Eucharist takes transubstantiation to its logical conclusion.[10] And this leads to a more serious problem: It gives the appearance of worshiping created things instead of the Creator. Even if we concede the logical consistency, Christ gave no instruction to worship Him under the guise of food and drink. This overwhelms the mystery.

Consubstantiation: The Lutheran Claim

Lutherans, on the other hand, teach the doctrine of *consubstantiation* (lit. "with the substance").[11] Several early church fathers (*e.g.* Ignatius of Antioch and Justin Martyr) affirmed a local presence of Christ in the sacrament.[12] Yet Martin Luther developed this further, maintaining a clearer distinction between sign and

---

[10] Eastern Orthodoxy rejects the necessity of this conclusion. This tradition reserves the sacrament for the sick, rather than setting it apart for adoration. See Ware, *Orthodox Church*, 285.

[11] It is important to note that Lutherans themselves may not use this term. Nevertheless, their position affirms the true and substantial presence of Christ's body and blood together with the bread and wine.

[12] Schaff, *History*, 2:241-42.

reality than transubstantiation: The bread and the wine continue to be sensory objects, but with the added presence of Christ "in, with, and under."[13]

Yet consubstantiation still has some weaknesses. Like transubstantiation, the first weakness involves the words of institution. The Lutheran view teaches that Christ's body and blood are in, with, and under the bread and wine. Yet, our Lord didn't say, "This *accompanies* my body"; He declared, "This *is*."[14]

This view is also burdened by a more serious problem: The omnipresence of Christ's human body. Lutherans believe that our Lord is present both in his deity and in his humanity during every Supper, everywhere at the same time.[15] But in their desire to be objective, they created an unnecessary dilemma concerning the two

---

[13] *Luther's Small Catechism with Explanation* (St. Louis: Concordia, 2017), 323: "We confess that we receive the very body and blood of Christ—in, with, and under the bread and wine—in our hands and in our mouths."

[14] Regarding the words of institution, Lutherans believe "this is" *means* "this is" rather than "this accompanies." However, they recognize that the bread and wine *contain* the body and blood. According to Rev Christopher Neuendorf of the Lutheran Church Missouri Synod, "They are the vehicle through which Jesus' body and blood are shared out among His people."

[15] Martin Luther, "The Sacrament of the Body and Blood of Christ—Against the Fanatics" in *Luther's Works, American Edition* (vols. 1–30; ed. Jaroslav Pelikan [St. Louis: Concordia, 1955–76]; vols. 31–55; ed. Helmut Lehmann [Philadelphia/Minneapolis: Muhlenberg/Fortress, 1957–86]; vols. 56–82; ed. Christopher Boyd Brown and Benjamin T. G. Mayes [St. Louis: Concordia, 2009–]), 36:342: "We believe that Christ, according to his human nature, is put over all creatures [Eph. 1:22] and fills all things, as Paul says in Eph. 4 [:10]. Not only according to his divine nature, but also according to his human nature, he is lord over all things, has all things in his hand, and is present everywhere."

natures of Christ. Jesus took on human nature when He was conceived in the womb of the virgin (Lk. 1:35). He experienced everything we experience, except for sin (Mt.4:2; Jn. 19:28; Heb. 4:15). Yet His human nature isn't omnipresent; it's fixed in a place. When Jesus ascended into heaven, He left one place and entered into another (Luke 12:51). So Jesus in His humanity can't be present everywhere—or at every Lord's Table. If He were, it would compromise His humanity.

Moreover, if Christ's body is everywhere, He can't represent His people. First Corinthians 15:20-23 describes Christ's resurrection as the *first fruits* (*i.e.* first yield) of many resurrections. This means His glorified body guarantees our future glorified bodies (Phil. 3:21). But if Christ is the first fruits and his glorified body is omnipresent, then our future glorified bodies would also be omnipresent. This would compromise *our* humanity. Since He had to be made like us in every way to serve as our high priest (Heb. 2:17), His humanity and ours are inseparably linked. Therefore, consubstantiation adds an unfortunate wrinkle to the mystery.

Due to the local presence of Christ in the sacrament, Lutherans also teach that the real presence is received by believers and unbelievers alike.[16] This claim will be challenged in the next section as we consider the Reformed alternative.

Spiritual Presence: The Reformed Alternative

We've seen how the Roman Catholic and Lutheran views fall short of preserving the mystery of the sacramental union. So what's the alternative? The

---

[16] Formula of Concord, Article VII in Schaff, *Creeds*, 2:140

answer comes from the other branch of the Reformation. The Reformed view differs from the other views by emphasizing the role of the Holy Spirit in preserving the mystery. This is why it's is called the *spiritual* real presence view.

The Reformed view had early proponents in Augustine, Ratramnus, and Berengar, but it's best known advocate was John Calvin, whose view is reflected in Reformed and Presbyterian standards.[17]

To begin, the Reformed view must be understood through the concept of *covenant*.[18] Elsewhere, I've defined a covenant as a "legal relationship."[19] In the Bible, when God entered into covenant with his people, He often reminded them of His saving deeds. Yet biblical covenants aren't only symbolic acts of remembrance. There's a close relationship between the sign and the covenant it represents. God called circumcision "my covenant" (Gen. 17:10), while Jesus termed the cup "the new covenant in my blood" (Lk.

---

[17] John Calvin, *Institutes of the Christian Religion* (2 vols.; ed. John T. McNeil; trans. Ford Lewis Battles; Library of Christian Classics; Philadelphia: The Westminster Press; London: S.C.M. Press, 1960), 2:1359-61 in which he referred to the sacrament as "a spiritual feast" and a "great mystery." *cf.* Heidelberg Catechism (HC) Q 76, WCF 29.7.

Note: This shouldn't be confused with the view of Ulrich Zwingli, an earlier Reformed theologian who debated Luther on the sacrament. Zwingli held a symbolic view of the Supper, emphasizing our remembrance while minimizing the real presence (See Schaff, *History*, 7:676-78).

[18] WCF 27.1.

[19] Ken Golden, *Presbytopia: What it means to be Presbyterian* (repr.; Ross-shire, UK: Christian Focus, 2017), 122.

22:20).[20] There's also a close connection between the sign used and the reality given. When Jesus declared, "This is the new covenant in my blood", He was neither transforming the wine into His blood nor situating Himself in, with, and under it. Instead, He was connecting His death and its benefits to the wine and its partakers.

This touches on the mystery of the sacramental union, and here it is important to discuss the role of the Holy Spirit. Christ's humanity is found in heaven, and we are bound to the earth. And yet the Spirit connects heaven and earth, bringing Jesus to us and us to Him (Jn. 14:26; 16:13-14). This is what it means to be in union with, or simply, *in* Christ. In Christ, we are made into a new creation (2 Cor. 5:17), experience no condemnation (Rom. 8:1), receive forgiveness (Eph. 1:7), and acquire every spiritual blessing (Eph. 1:3). But 1 John 4:13 reveals the mediator of our union with Christ: "By this we know that we abide in Him and He in us, because He has given us of His Spirit."

The Spirit mediates union with Christ through word and sacrament. God's people are commended when the word abides in them (1 Jn. 2:14). In baptism, Christians "put on Christ" (Gal. 3:27) and are baptized into one body through one Spirit (1 Cor. 12:13). Likewise, the Lord's Supper is described as a

---

[20] Michael Horton, *The Christian Faith* (Grand Rapids: Zondervan, 2011), 782: "Clearly, these covenantal actions are not merely illustrations. Yet they are also not a magical transformation of earthly substances into divine substances. Rather they are performative actions that do what they say. In and through the act of consecrating bread and wine as his body and blood, Jesus hands himself over to death as the sacrifice for the sins of those who eat and drink in faith."

participation (or fellowship, *koinonia*) with the body and blood of Christ (1 Cor. 10:16). Jesus declared, "Whoever feeds on my flesh and drinks my blood abides in me and I in him" (Jn. 6:56). While feeding can mean *believing*, it can also describe partaking of the sacrament. Thus, the Spirit uses the Supper to deepen our union with Christ.

While both the Roman Catholics and Lutherans value union with Christ, they require that Christ descends to us. The Reformed believe the opposite; rather than Christ coming down, the Spirit raises us up to Christ and seats us in the heavenly places (Eph. 2:6; Col 3:1). Ours is a fellowship with the incarnate Christ. His humanity is circumscribed to a place, available by the Spirit, and received by faith.

This is why the Reformed disagree with the Lutherans about the objective reception of the Lord's Supper. If the Spirit mediates union with Christ through the sacrament, then only believers can receive the reality. Unbelievers would receive the signs without any spiritual advantage to their souls.

Most importantly, the spiritual real presence view preserves the mystery of the sacramental union. John Calvin affirmed this in the most eloquent words:

> Now if anyone should ask me how this takes place, I shall not be ashamed to confess that it is a secret too lofty for either my mind to comprehend or my words to declare. And to speak more plainly, I rather experience than understand it. Therefore, I here embrace without controversy the truth of God in which I may safely rest. He declares his flesh the food of my soul, his blood its drink [Jn. 6:53 ff.]. I offer my soul to him to be fed with such food. In his Sacred Supper he bids me to take, eat, and drink his body

and blood under the symbols of bread and wine. I do not doubt that he himself truly presents them, and that I receive them.[21]

The spiritual presence view upholds the sacramental mystery without replacing the earthly signs or compromising the heavenly realty. In this way, the integrity of the sacrament union is maintained, and partakers can be assured they are receiving Christ in the Supper.

---

[21] Calvin, *Institutes*, 2:1403-4.

Chapter Three

Family Expectations

Different meals have different expectations. Fast food take-out can be eaten in front of the television or even on the ride home. You can eat as quickly as you like, with or without utensils, and with minimal social interaction.

Family meals are different. They carry more expectations, things like table manners and social interaction. They assume you're part of the social structure called "the family."

This is also true for *spiritual* family meals. The Lord invites us to His Table. He's prepared a covenant meal offering heavenly blessings through earthly food and drink. But covenants are two-sided. Christ has fulfilled the covenant requirements so that we can dine at His table, but we must still respond. Conditions must still be met. In ecclesiastical circles, this is called "fencing the table", but for the purpose of this book, we'll call it *family expectations*. This chapter focuses on the family expectations that are required for us to participate in the sacrament.

Baptism: Joining the Family

In order to be part of the family meal, one must first join the family. For Christians this happens through the sacrament of baptism. Like all sacraments, baptism involves the union of a sign (water) with a reality (new life, remission of sins, union with Christ). In the Old Testament, water was used for purifying clergy and laity alike as they approached God in the Tabernacle and Temple (Ex. 30:17-21; 2 Chr. 4:6; Num. 8:5-7; Lev. 14-15). This purification later became connected to rebirth (Ezek. 36:25-26) which explained the new life expressed in baptism (Jn. 3:5; Tit. 3:5; Heb. 10:22). The purpose of washing was for the remission of sins (Isa. 1:16) which was linked to both John's baptism (Lk. 3:3) and Christian baptism (Acts 2:38).

Yet baptism is best known as the sacrament of *initiation*. It's the gateway into the church. This was the function of circumcision in the Old Testament. In Genesis 17:9-14, God told Abraham that His covenant involved the circumcision of every male. This brought all the household males into the covenant community and set them apart for holiness. Yet circumcision wasn't a bare sign; it was connected to the "circumcision of the heart" (Deut. 30:6; Jer. 4:4), the Old Testament equivalent of new life and union with God. In the New Testament, baptism has replaced circumcision as the sacrament of inclusion and union (Mt.28:19; Col. 2:11-12). Paul wrote, "For in one Spirit we were all baptized into one body" (1 Cor. 12:13).

What does this have to do with the Lord's Supper? Given the parallels between circumcision and baptism, we discover that sacrament of joining God's family must precede the sacrament of partaking the family meal. In Exodus 12:45, a foreigner could not eat the Passover until he was circumcised. Just as only those who formally had entered into Israel could partake of the Passover, so only those who formally enter the church can partake of the Passover's fulfillment. Since the Lord's Supper is the family meal of the church, one needs to join the family before partaking.

Membership: Taking Your Place

Yet Baptism is only the beginning. Participation in the Lord's Supper also requires active membership in the visible church. Some churches call this "confirmation," others "public profession of faith." But this requires some explanation. Here it's helpful to distinguish the "invisible" church from the "visible" church. The invisible church "consists of the whole number of the elect that have been, are, or shall be gathered into one, under Christ the Head" (Eph. 1:22-23; Heb. 12:22-23). [1]This is the church of all times and places, the people we'll enjoy everlasting fellowship with. The problem is we don't know who these people are. We accept people based on their credible profession of faith which may or may not be a window into election. Some are self-deceived and make false professions; only God knows for sure.

But the visible church is broader. This church "consists of all those throughout the world that profess the true religion and of their children" (Rom. 1:7; 1 Cor. 1:2; Acts 16:30-33; 1 Cor. 1:16).[2] It contains a portion of the invisible church, but also false members and those who've yet to profess their faith. For example, Paul

---

[1] WCF 25.1.

[2] WCF 25.2.

addressed the Church of Corinth as saints (1:2) even though some of them were promoting factions (3:1-9), approving a sinful marriage (5:1-2), and denying the resurrection (15:12-19)! Our visible congregations have more in common with Corinth than we realize.

What does this have to do with the Lord's Supper? We've already seen how 1 Corinthians 10:16 describes the sacrament as fellowship in the body and blood of Christ. Now let's consider the next verse: "Because there is one bread, we who are many are one body, for we all partake of the one bread." Here, the body is the visible church with all its sins and struggles. Yet Paul addressed them as saints, those who entered through baptism, became members, and were striving to live holy lives. They have access to the "one bread" because they are part of the "one body." They're members of Christ through His visible church.

The Reformed tradition does not regard itself as the *only* body. Presbyterians don't believe that any one branch of the visible church has cornered the market on truth. Rather, all are subject to "mixture and error."[3] Yet all churches that teach the Gospel are considered members of the larger visible church. We welcome such members and invite them to the Lord's table.

But sometimes our churches receive visitors who claim to be part of the invisible church while not being members of a visible church. Some are in transition, searching for a new church home. Others may not be

---

[3] WCF 25.4: "This [universal] church has been sometimes more, sometimes less visible. And particular churches, which are members thereof, are more or less pure, according as the doctrine of the gospel is taught and embraced, ordinances administered, and public worship performed more or less purely in them."

ready or willing to submit themselves to the oversight of a local congregation. Yet the Lord's Supper is a visible church ordinance. For that reason, only members of a visible church in good standing should be allowed to partake.

Preparation: Eating and Drinking Responsibly

Participation requires more than simply baptism and membership in a visible church; it also involves *preparation*. In 1 Corinthians 11:27-29, Paul discussed this under three headings: Worthy partaking, self-examination, and discerning the body.

First, the apostle warned, "Whoever, therefore, eats the bread or drinks the cup of the Lord in an unworthy manner will be guilty concerning the body and blood of the Lord" (v. 27). What does this mean? Everyone is unworthy by the simple fact that everyone is a sinner. Yet the sacrament is still offered to sinners striving to be saints. Rather than describing a merit-based worthiness, Paul was focusing on *public* worthiness. In vv. 17-22 the apostle rebuked the church. Their divisions were spilling over into the sacrament and its accompanying love feasts. Some were left hungry, humiliated by their fellow members.[4] Others got drunk. How could they celebrate the "one bread" when they weren't acting like "one body" (10:17)? Paul

---

[4] *Cf.* Mathison, *Given For You*, 230: "In the first century Roman Empire, it was also customary for a host to keep the best food for himself and those guests who belonged to the upper classes. The lesser food and scraps of the better food would go to the lower-class guests. If this is what was going on in Corinth, Paul's words are understandable. The rich members of the church were showing contempt for the poor members of the church. In showing contempt for any member of the body of Christ, they were showing contempt for Christ himself."

went as far as to say, "When you come together, it is
not the Lord's supper that you eat" (v. 20). That's quite
an indictment! They were consuming the outward
food, but not the heavenly reality. It's hard to imagine
this happening in the twenty-first century church, yet
our modern-day congregations also struggle with
division and partiality. We need to make sure we're
partaking worthily.

Second, the apostle said, "Let a person examine
himself, then, and so eat of the bread and drink of the
cup" (v. 28). Unlike worthy partaking, self-examination
is a private matter. Each Christian must take personal
inventory before coming to the table. But this raises
some questions. How much self-examination is
necessary? Where does one draw the line? Some who
are overly self-critical may excuse themselves from the
sacrament altogether. Burdened by tender consciences
and unrealistic expectations, their introspection can
lead to despair. But this wasn't the apostle's goal. This
sacrament isn't a prize for the virtuous; it's fuel for
overcomers! Christ offers Himself to struggling sinners,
not perfected saints.

Self-examination needs to be informed by Scripture. In
the Sermon on the Mount, Jesus spoke against sinful
anger as the root of murder. "So if you are offering
your gift at the altar and there remember that your
brother has something against you, leave your gift
there before the altar and go. First be reconciled to your
brother, and then come and offer your gift" (Mt.
5:24-25). Why would Jesus mention the altar? Because
in the old covenant, that was the place an Israelite went
to be reconciled with God. However, the Lord wasn't
interested in empty sacrifices. He desired the sacrifices
to match the sincerity of the sacrificer. So Jesus

provided some guidance: before seeking reconciliation with God, seek reconciliation with each other. You can't force reconciliation, but you can make the effort. Even if reaching the other person is unrealistic, you can *desire* reconciliation.[5] If sinful anger is the root of murder, then removing the sinful anger is an expression of love. What are you bringing to the Lord's table? Sinful anger, bitterness, hatred? Deal with it first. Then come and partake of the meal that assumes reconciliation with God.

Self-examination also doesn't exclude the decisions of church officers. The church still has a responsibility to judge its own, especially when its members are blind to their sins. Earlier in First Corinthians, Paul addressed a flagrant case of sexual immorality. He wrote, "But now I am writing to you not to associate with anyone who bears the name of brother if he is guilty of sexual immorality or greed, or is an idolater, reviler, drunkard, or swindler—*not even to eat with such a one*" (1 Cor. 5:11, emphasis added). The sinner may have been incapable of examining himself, so the church needed to intervene in order to preserve its peace and purity.

Finally, Paul cautioned, "For anyone who eats and drinks without discerning the body eats and drinks judgment on himself" (v. 29). The question is, *"Which body?"* Was he referring to Christ's risen body in the sacrament (1 Cor. 11:24) or His spiritual body in the

---

[5] David E. Garland, *Reading Matthew: A Literary and Theological Commentary* (Macon, GA: Smyth & Helwys, 2001), 66: "It would be inconceivable for Galileans, for example, to halt sacrificial proceedings, to return to Galilee, to search out the offended person and do whatever is necessary to bring about reconciliation, and then to return to the temple in Jerusalem and pick up the sacrifice where they had left off."

church (1 Cor. 10:17; *cf.* 12:13)? The first requires *doctrinal* understanding: Partakers need to grasp the meaning of the Lord's Supper and other basic teachings. The second involves *relational* understanding: Participants need to see themselves as part of a larger community. These options aren't mutually exclusive. Preparation requires knowing what we believe and how that knowledge affects community living.

These aren't trivial matters. Members of the Corinthian church were judged for their lack of preparation (1 Cor. 11:30-31). It's safe to say their judgment was extraordinary; we shouldn't fear for our lives every time we come to the table. Yet it demonstrates the gravity of communion and the necessity of preparation.

This is something the twenty-first church needs to remember. In place of division, we should seek harmony. Instead of carelessness, we should practice self-examination. Rather than ignorance, we should pursue discernment. Then we'll be prepared to eat and drink responsibly.

Chapter Four

Frequent Feeding

The question of frequency—how often or seldom we do something—isn't a trivial matter. This is true about consumption. How often should we eat and drink? Most of us partake three times per day. Some prefer smaller quantities more often, while others gorge themselves at every meal. Still others diet to their peril, malnourished in their self-denial. Our bodies need food and drink to survive, the right amount to thrive.

The same goes for spiritual consumption. Our souls also need food and drink, the right amount to thrive. God provides His sacrament, but how often should we partake? Should observance be frequent or occasional? Should the Lord's Supper be a regular part of worship?

In fourth petition of the Lord's Prayer, we're taught to pray, "give us this day our daily bread" (Mt. 6:11). This concerns our daily *needs* rather than wants. Some traditions provide a daily sacrament because they see it as a need. Others offer it far less often for a variety of reasons. Chapter Four makes the case for a *frequent and regular* celebration of the Lord's Supper. Preferably, this would happen as often as the church is required to meet for worship: Once every Lord's Day. In support of this frequency, the present chapter will survey the biblical data, offer theological reasons, and answer potential objections.[1]

Biblical Data

Jesus instituted the Lord's Supper during his last Passover on earth. The next reference to the sacrament followed Pentecost when 3000 people were baptized. "And they devoted themselves to the apostles' teaching and the fellowship, to the breaking of bread and the prayers" (Acts 2:42). This text lists out normal elements of worship. How do we know this? For starters, each item has a definite article: *The* apostle's teaching, *the* fellowship, *the* breaking of bread, *the* prayers. These are specific things done in worship. The apostles' teaching consisted of preaching and teaching (Rom. 10:14-17). The fellowship (*koinonia*) involved offerings for the needy (Acts 2:44-45; cf. 2 Cor. 9:13 in which *koinonia* is translated as "contribution"). The prayers were spoken in community (Acts 12:12). And the breaking of bread expressed both table fellowship (Acts 2:46) and a specific ritual, the Lord's Supper.

We also know the breaking of bread is sacramental by its usage in Luke/Acts. In Luke 24:13-35, two disciples

---

[1] This chapter assumes that biblical exegesis rather than church tradition is the basis for this requirement. Consequently, I argue for one Lord's Supper administration on the Lord's Day because there is no explicit biblical evidence for more than this frequency. Some would argue for two services, but this is more beneficial than essential. The old covenant requirement of morning and evening sacrifices (Num. 28:1-10; Ps. 92:1-2) is suggestive rather than binding for all times and places. These sacrifices were types and shadows that found their fulfillment in Christ (Col. 2:16-17). And while having a second service can be useful in sanctifying the Lord's Day, it's an *application* of a biblical principle which requires the use of biblical wisdom.

were returning to Emmaus, mourning of the death of their master. Along the way, they met a stranger—the risen Savior—even though they didn't recognize Him. As they traveled, He explained how the Old Testament pointed to His death and resurrection. Upon reaching Emmaus, they urged Him to dine with them. But once at the table, the guest became the host. He took bread, blessed and broke it, and gave it to them just like He did at the Last Supper. In doing so, their eyes were opened and they finally recognized Him. He revealed himself *specifically* through the breaking of bread. This made the meal sacramental.

Another compelling example is found in Acts 20:7, 11:

> On the first day of the week, when we were gathered together to break bread, Paul talked with them, intending to depart the next day and he prolonged his speech until midnight... And when Paul had gone up and had broken bread and eaten, he conversed with them a long while, until daybreak, and so departed.

Here, Luke wrote about an evening worship service in Troas with emphasis on teaching and "breaking of bread." A few details are worth noting.

First, "gathered together" is a form of the verb *sunago* related to the noun *sunagoge* from which we get "synagogue." This describes communal activity or worship. And not just worship in general, but the celebration of the Supper! According to v. 7, they were gathered for the *purpose* of breaking bread.[2] Second,

---

[2] T. David Gordon, "Why Weekly Communion," *Ordained Servant* 17 (2008): 109: "The implication is not that they did nothing else on the Lord's Day, but that the Lord's Supper so *characterized* their assembly that it could accurately be designated as a gathering "to break bread."

this text is more time-specific than Acts 2:42 with its mention of the first day. This follows the pattern of the New Testament church gathering on the first day (Lord's Day) instead of the seventh day (Sabbath). Rather than the daily observance found in Acts 2:42, we find the celebration taking place on the Lord's Day. Third, the Lord's Supper is in view because v. 11 contains the definite article and the meal follows the preaching of the word. This echoes the theme of word and sacrament together.

Besides Luke/Acts, we also find evidence for frequent communion in Paul's writing. Here, we return to a text discussed in the previous chapter.

> But in the following instructions I do not commend you, because when you come together it is not for the better but for the worse. For in the first place, when you come together as a church, I hear that there are divisions among you. . . . When you come together, it is not the Lord's Supper that you eat (1 Cor. 11:17-20).

As we previously learned, Paul was addressing sacramental abuses in the Corinthian church. Yet the details also shed light on the present subject. While verses 17, 18, 20 utilize a different verb (*sunerchomai*) than Acts 20:7 (*sunago*), they still describe the church "coming together." In v. 20, when the church met together, they were outwardly taking the sacrament, but inwardly destroying the unity. Their motives were selfish instead of communal. Yet v. 20 explicitly says they were receiving the sacrament *when they came together*. The obvious conclusion is that the sacrament was celebrated whenever they congregated! This text not only establishes frequency in 1 Corinthians, but also clarifies Acts 20.[3] Like the rest of the key New Testament texts, v. 20 supports rather than impedes frequent administration of the sacrament.

1 Corinthians 11:26 is often used as a counterpoint to frequent communion. Supporters of less-frequent communion would argue that the phrase, "as often as you drink it" is ambiguous about frequency. However, the context of chapter 11 dictates the meaning of the disputed phrase. "As often as you drink it" would occur "when you come together" (v. 20).

Theological Reasons

Besides the Biblical data, there are sound theological reasons for frequent communion. First, the Lord's Supper is a means of grace. Chapter one argued that the sacrament is "soul food and spiritual drink" based on Melchizedek's ceremony (Gen. 14:18-20), the Passover/Last Supper rituals (Exod. 12, synoptic Last Supper accounts), the manna/bread of life discourse (Exod. 16, Jn. 6), and the contrasting spiritual/demonic tables (1 Cor. 10). If the sacrament is a means of spiritual growth, then why limit the opportunities to receive it?[4] Since Paul calls it fellowship with the body

---

[3] Both Acts 20 and 1 Corinthians 10 and 11 share similar language. The former includes "we were gathered together to break of bread" (v.7) while the latter mentions "when you come together" (11:20) and "the bread we break" (10:16). Since 1 Corinthians falls in the timeline of Acts 19, Paul's statements precede the events of Acts 20:7. It is then likely that Acts 20:7 describes the sacrament in the regular gathering of the church on the first day of the week.

[4] W. Robert Godfrey, "Calvin on the Eucharist", *Modern Reformation,* May/June 1997: "The frequency of administration may say something about what we expect to find at that table (or, maybe I should say, whom we expect to find at that table) and what the blessing of meeting Jesus Christ there really is."

and blood of Christ (1 Cor. 10:16), we should seek such fellowship as often as possible.

There's good reason for doing this, since the New Testament shows a connection between word and sacrament (Lk. 24:30-32, 34; Acts 2:42, 20:7, 11). While it's true the word is primary and the sacrament secondary, that doesn't mean the latter should be optional. Except in extraordinary situations when it's not possible to administer the sacrament, the two are meant to go together.

Finally, there's another compelling reason for frequent communion. Besides providing participants with spiritual food and drink, the sacrament also "put[s] a visible difference between those that belong unto the church, and the rest of the world."[5] This is something that even the reading and preaching word doesn't do. Both believers and unbelievers may read the Bible and listen to a sermon, but only believers are allowed to receive the sacrament.[6] Being barred from the sacrament week after week may harden some people. Yet it is a witness to those who are on the fence. Perhaps they'll start asking themselves, "What am I missing?" If so, we can provide a ready answer: Intimate communion with our risen Savior who nourishes us with His body and blood.

Answering Objections

Not everyone is persuaded about frequent communion. In discussing the 1 Corinthians text, I already answered

---

[5] WCF 27:1.

[6] Gordon, "Weekly," 110-11.

one biblical objection. Now we'll consider some other objections in the balance of this chapter.

1. The Relationship to the Passover. This objection insists on consistency in spiritual meals. Since the Old Testament Passover was an annual event, its New Testament fulfillment should also be an annual event. Yet this ignores the multi-faceted nature of the sacrament. It not only fulfills the annual Passover, but also Melchizedek's ceremony (Gen. 14:18-20), the old covenant peace offerings (Lev. 7) and the daily manna in the wilderness (Ex. 16; Jn. 6).

2. The Crypto-Catholic argument. This objection argues guilt by association. Since the Roman Catholic Church practices frequent (even daily) communion, Protestants should avoid this practice. Yet this is a logical fallacy. Roman Catholics and Protestants have other shared beliefs, such as the Trinity, the deity of Christ, and original sin. It would be absurd to disown essential Christian doctrines because a different church holds to them. The same holds for frequent communion. The Bible, rather than church tradition, informs our practice.

3. Trivializes the Sacrament. According to this objection, the more we celebrate the sacrament, the more we'll take it for granted and go through the motions. While this is a potential danger, any part of the liturgy could become trivialized by our wandering minds. Worship is a discipline as well as a blessing.

4. Lengthens Worship Service. This pragmatic objection assumes the longer the worship service, the less focused we become. There might actually be some truth to this. Worship is a blessing to God's people, but they also live in a culture that cultivates short attention spans. So conducting a two hour worship service may not be the best way to keep a congregation focused. Yet shortening the service doesn't have to involve infrequent communion. Other elements of worship could be shortened to accommodate the concern about time. This even applies to the preaching of the word. Sermons don't have to be long to be effective.

5. *Requires Preparation.* According to this objection, the sacrament requires self-examination ahead of time, so frequent administration does not offer adequate preparation. Chapter 3 addressed the issue of biblical preparation from 1 Corinthians 11:27-29. It's true that partakers must examine themselves before coming to the table, but Paul doesn't specify a timeframe. Self-examination is a daily discipline that shouldn't impact the frequency of administration.

6. *Unity of the Broader Church.* This objection is concerned that frequent communion can become a divisive practice in denominations or families of churches that practice less frequent communion.[7] It's possible for those accustomed to frequent communion to look down upon those who oppose it. That's the essence of

---

[7] So Todd Bordow, "Rethinking Weekly Communion," *Ordained Servant* 17 (May 2008): 106. The author specifically addressed the practice of weekly communion and raised some important points. For example: "One wonders whether the weekly communion proponents have considered the ramifications of their views on their members who relocate. In our mobile society it is likely a majority of our members will need to change churches at least once in their lives. If these members have been convinced that weekly communion is both biblical and necessary for the feeding of their souls, they will have a difficult time finding a church in an area where the Reformed or conservative Presbyterians do not practice weekly communion. ... They will also be tempted to disparage good churches that would greatly benefit them simply because those churches do not share the same frequency conviction."

spiritual pride! Yet responsible churches will teach their members to show charity towards different views. Moreover, if taken to its logical conclusion, this objection would also rule out the use of fermented wine, creedal recitation, and other practices that have latitude in a family of churches.

7. *Compromises the Outreach of the Church.* According to this objection, the practice of frequent communion serves as an unnecessary obstacle for inquirers who already have to overcome the unique distinctives of a confessional tradition.[8] While it's conceded that churches need to use wisdom in implementing changes, such wisdom is formed by discerning the likeliest teaching of Scripture. Any visitor who's convinced that the Bible is the word of God and that preaching and sacraments are means of strengthening faith, should at least be willing to consider the arguments for frequent communion.

8. *Compromises the Primacy of the Word.* Finally, this objection assumes that the more the sacrament is celebrated, the more the word will be supplanted. This is the weightiest objection of all. Certainly the word is prior to the sacrament, the latter depending on the former. So the church must guard against this tendency found in other traditions. Yet ironically, infrequent communion can create the same problem. The concept of "Communion Sunday" can lead people to exalt the sacrament as something "special." This runs of risk of seeing the ordinary parts of worship as "less special", including the preaching of the word.

---

[8] Bordow, "Rethinking," 106-7.

In the final analysis, none of these objections are persuasive enough to overturn the biblical data and theological benefits of frequent communion on the Lord's Day. Just as the Lord taught his disciples to ask for their daily bread, the twenty-first century Christians should petition their churches for their "frequent bread."

Chapter Five

Menu Options – Bread

Food is a source of comfort, and specific foods have universal appeal. As a well-known Spanish proverb that says, "All griefs with bread are less." For many centuries, this hearty staple has satisfied the young and old, rich and poor, joyful and sad.

Of all the foods to describe his physical suffering, Jesus chose bread. He broke it, shared it, and used it to fulfill the old covenant. By eating bread, His disciples learned that He is the ultimate source of comfort. All griefs with Jesus are less.

Bread is an essential part of the Lord's Supper. The Bible mentions two basic kinds: Unleavened and leavened. Which one should be used? This chapter presents a biblical case for each of these "menu options," but the results are not conclusive. In the final analysis, Scripture doesn't specify the type of bread that must be used in the sacrament and arguments can be made for both kinds. As in all things, wisdom must be employed when making this decision.

The Case for Unleavened Bread

Unleavened bread has ancient roots in the Old Testament. The first reference precedes the giving of the law at Sinai. As the Israelites wandered the wilderness, God fed them *manna*—unleavened bread from heaven. This was the "spiritual food" of the Exodus generation. (1 Cor. 10:3). Yet the most well-known example of unleavened bread is found in the Passover story (Exod. 12). God commanded Israel to eat the meal in haste with belts secured, sandals fastened, and staves in hand (v. 11). This hurriedness also affected the bread since there was no time for leaven. They needed to eat in a hurry; their unleavened bread reflected the urgency of their deliverance.

This wasn't a one-time event. The Lord commanded Israel to observe an ongoing festival so that future generations would remember this deliverance (v.17). The first day would be an annual celebration of the Passover, while the next six days rounded out the Feast of Unleavened Bread. This festival would become the first of the three pilgrim feasts. Each required the male Israelites to make pilgrimage to God's appointed place (Exod. 23:16; Deut. 16:16) which found a permanent location in Jerusalem (Isa. 33:20; Lk. 2:41-42).

During his last Passover on earth, Jesus followed the old covenant stipulations. This means the bread of the Last Supper had to be unleavened, and some cite this as evidence for using it in the Lord's Supper today. Unleavened bread was also used in the sacrifices of the Tabernacle and Temple. Grain offerings had to be unleavened loaves mixed or smeared with oil (Lev. 2:4), and animal sacrifices couldn't be offered with anything leavened (Ex. 23:8).

These requirements raise the question, "What's wrong with leavened bread?" To answer this, we need to understand the definition and purpose of leaven.

Leaven old, fermented dough that causes other dough to change. Leaven works through the entire lump, changing every part as it spreads.

Besides commemorating the haste of the Exodus, unleavened bread also reminded Israel of the need for ongoing purity. God saved His people for a specific reason: To shape them into a kingdom of priests and a holy nation (Ex. 19:6) that would be a light to all the nations (Isa. 49:6). To fulfill this mission, Israel needed to be pure. The leaven of idolatry needed to be avoided so it wouldn't spread through the dough.

The New Testament also mentions leaven as a negative metaphor. Jesus used it to describe the influential (and hypocritical) tradition of the Pharisees (Mt. 16:6, 11-12; Mk. 8:15; Lk. 12:1). Paul also utilized it to portray the heresy of the Judaizers (Gal. 5:9) and address an immoral situation in the church of Corinth. Concerning the latter, he wrote:

> Cleanse out the old leaven that you may be a new lump, as you really are unleavened. For Christ, our Passover lamb, has been sacrificed. Let us therefore celebrate the festival, not with the old leaven, the leaven of malice and evil, but with the unleavened bread of sincerity and truth (1 Cor. 5:7-8).

Here Paul connects the Corinthian church to the Exodus generation. Like Israel set apart for holiness, he referred to them as "a new lump" of unleavened dough. He contrasted the leaven which represents vice ("malice and evil") with unleavened bread which represents virtue ("sincerity and truth"). These virtues weren't inherent in the Corinthians, but accessed through their union with Christ. As the blood of lambs protected the Israelites from the tenth plague (Ex. 12:5,

7. 12-13), so the blood of Christ—the ultimate Passover Lamb (Jn. 1:29)—covers the sins of His people (Rom. 5:9; 1 Pet. 1:18-19).

The Case for Leavened Bread

The argument for unleavened bread is strong, yet this isn't an open-and-shut case. Those in favor of leaven in the Lord's Supper can find support from the biblical meaning of "bread," the weight of New Testament discontinuity, and the positive use of leaven.

The Bible describes bread as a staple of life, a common blessing for all people (2 Kgs. 18:32; Ps. 104:15; Eccl. 9:7). Psalm 104, a creation song, praises God as provider of man's basic needs. Along with wine and oil, bread is given to "strengthen man's heart" (v. 15).

This common staple was also used for spiritual purposes. The priest-king Melchizedek, a type and shadow of Christ, mediated God's blessings to Abraham through the use of bread (Gen. 14:18). And Christ himself used bread to reveal himself to his disciples (Lk. 24:31; Jn. 21:12-14). While the Luke 24 reference fell under the time frame of unleavened bread, the John 21 reference fell outside of that festival. It described a common meal that Christ transformed for spiritual purposes—and there's nothing in the text that suggests the bread was unleavened.[1]

Proponents of unleavened bread make a strong case for continuity with the Old Testament, but the opposite case can be made for *discontinuity* in the New Testament. Appealing to the Last Supper narratives for the ongoing use of unleavened bread has its merits, but remember that the meal in the upper room was still a Passover meal. Indeed, it was the last Passover from the standpoint of redemptive history. During that meal, Jesus fulfilled the old covenant while ratifying the new (Luke 22:20). One could argue that the unleavened bread was as much a part of the old covenant as the sacrifices it accompanied. In that case, it would fall under the types and shadows that were fulfilled in Christ (Col. 2:16-17). Even though the Lord's Supper is a renewal of the new covenant ratified at the Last Supper, it doesn't necessarily require the same form of the bread.

The Bible even has some positive things to say about leaven. In the Old Testament, it was used in the Tabernacle/Temple alongside the unleavened product. Not only was leavened bread acceptable for religious use, but it was specifically used with the peace

---

[1] Septuagint and New Testament use two Greek words for bread. *Azymos* described unleavened bread in the context of the Feast of Unleavened Bread and Levitical sacrifices of the Old Testament. Paul also used it in his metaphor of sincerity and truth (1 Cor. 5:8). On the other hand, *artos* is the generic word for bread., used to describe both bread that had to be unleavened (e.g., Ex. 16:15; Lev. 24:5; Last Supper narratives; Lk. 24:30) and bread more likely to be leavened (e.g., Gen. 3:19; Eccl 9:7; Psa. 104:15; Jn. 21:13). Context would determine the meaning. After the Last Supper accounts, all references to bread in the Lord's Supper use *artos*.

offerings, an Old Testament precursor to the Lord's Supper (Lev. 7:13), since it was shared with priests and offeror (Lev. 7:19-21; 28-34). It was also used in the Feast of Weeks (Lev. 23:16-17) which found its fulfillment at Pentecost when the church experienced rapid growth (Acts 2).

The most positive statements about leaven come from the New Testament. In the Gospel of Matthew, Jesus uses leaven as a metaphor to describe the spread of His kingdom: "The kingdom of heaven is like leaven that a woman took and hid in three measures of flour till it was all leavened" (Mt. 13:33). Here there's nothing negative about the spread of leaven, but rather it symbolizes the spread of the kingdom from Jerusalem to Judea to Samaria to the ends of the earth (Acts 1:8). These Gentile areas knew hardly anything about Jewish ceremonial law. For them, leavened bread was a staple of life. In a Gentile context, using the unleavened bread might even be seen as a return to the types and shadows of the old covenant.

The Need for Wisdom

We've seen that cases can be made for both leavened and unleavened bread in the Lord's Supper. The old covenant required both kinds of bread for religious use. Leaven is used both positively and negatively in the Scriptures. The Last Supper was as an old covenant meal using unleavened bread, but the Lord's Supper is a new covenant meal with points of continuity and discontinuity.

So, which kind of bread should we use? We make that determination by exercising *wisdom*. This means subjecting our knowledge to biblical principles and common sense. Wisdom isn't "one size fits all"; it's often circumstantial. Different situations may require different answers.

A church's particular vision could inform this decision. Unleavened bread emphasizes continuity with old covenant, so traditions with deep roots in the Old Testament may favor this option. On the other hand, leavened bread pictures the extension of God's kingdom, and so mission-minded churches may prefer this option.

Aesthetics can also factor into decision-making. Some value the simplicity of a wafer, while others value the complexity of fresh artisan bread. Taste is another consideration. If the church with a vision for the community wants to emphasizing feeding, a hearty loaf may communicate this better than plain wafers.

There are also practical concerns. Fresh loaves become stale much faster than bland wafers. Cost must be considered, especially in larger congregations. And don't forget that congregants and visitors may have food allergies. Keeping a gluten free product on hand would add to the expense, yet providing for those with health concerns is an expression of Christian love, a worthy inclusion in the church budget.

Churches have the liberty to choose what makes the most sense in their context. The choice isn't set in stone. Menu options can change over time; wisdom, however, is always the best option.

Chapter Six

Menu Options — Wine

In the last chapter we discussed bread as a source of comfort; now we'll consider its liquid counterpart. There's a well-known Hebrew proverb that says, "No joy without wine." This pleasing drink has lifted the spirits of people for many centuries. Yet the joy of wine is often found in its complexity. Of all the beverages to describe His sacrificial death, Jesus chose wine. He gave thanks, poured it, and used it to fulfill the old covenant. By drinking wine, His disciples learned that He is the ultimate sacrifice for their sins. Their ultimate joy could only come through his blood.

Wine is also an essential part of the Lord's Supper. And yet this beverage comes with warnings, and Scripture's portrayal of wine is not always positive. This and other factors have led some in modern times to use unfermented wine (grape juice).

So which one should we use?

The unapologetic answer should be that *fermented* wine is the norm… but exceptions do exist. The obstacles of modern culture can affect the practices of the church. Concessions are sometimes necessary, though they should never replace the rule. This chapter presents the case for fermented wine, while allowing for the concession of unfermented grape juice.

The Case for Fermented Wine

Wine, like bread, is a *common* blessing for many cultures. Scripture confirms this in various ways. While bread strengthens the heart, wine "gladdens" it (Ps. 104:15; cf. Jdg. 9:13). It even has medicinal value. Paul advised Timothy, "No longer drink only water, but use a little wine for the sake of your stomach and your frequent ailments" (1 Tim. 5:23).

Wine is also a *covenant* blessing for God's people. It's often paired with other blessings such as grain and oil (Deut. 7:12-13; Jer. 31:11-12; Joel 2:19) and was part of the tithes that benefitted the nation (Deut. 14:22-23; Neh. 10:38-39). Yet the nation needed to be faithful to receive this blessing; the removal of wine was a part of the covenant curse (Deut. 28:39; Joel 1:10).

Wine was used in Old Testament worship. As he did with the bread, Melchizedek mediated God's blessings to Abraham through the use of wine (Gen. 14:18). This fermented beverage was later used in the old covenant drink offerings (Ex. 29:38-40; Lev. 23:13; Num. 15:5) and became part of the Passover liturgy. We see this in the Last Supper accounts.

Given this information, it should come as no surprise that Jesus drank wine. Christ's opponents certainly believed this, as He indicated when caricaturing their criticism: "The Son of Man came eating and drinking and they say, 'Look at him! A glutton and a drunkard, a friend of tax collectors and sinners'" (Mt. 11:19).

Could God in the flesh have be an alcoholic? Of course not! As Hebrews clearly teaches: "He was tempted every way has been tempted as we are, yet without sin" (Heb. 4:15). Yet even Christ's moderate drinking is shocking to Christians who demand total abstinence. Can our piety somehow exceed that of Jesus, who drank fermented wine?[1] The answer is again a resounding "No," especially in connection to the Lord's Supper.

But not everyone is convinced, and those opposed to fermented drink employ a number of counter-arguments. First, they point out that Last Supper accounts mention "fruit of the vine" rather than fermented wine (Mt. 26:29; Mk. 14:25; Lk. 22:18). This ambiguous phrase can also describe unfermented grapes. According to Zechariah 8:12: "The vine shall give its fruit, and the ground shall give its produce, and the heavens shall give their dew." Yet the prophet was speaking of covenant blessings in their respective infancies. For these to become covenant blessings, they must develop into wine, food, and rain.

Second, opponents claim that references to "new wine" describe the fruit of the vine before fermentation. Here, they point to the marriage of Cana where Jesus turned water into wine (John 2:1-11). The Bible, however, doesn't seem to support this theory. The Hebrew Old Testament used two words to describe wine: *yayen* ("wine") and *terosh* ("wine" or "new wine"). *Terosh* was often coupled with *dagan* ("grain") as products of agricultural fertility (Gen. 27:37; Deut. 7:13; Prov. 3:10; Jer. 31:12). So it's no surprise that pagan societies

---

[1] A. A. Hodge, *Evangelical Theology* (Edinburgh: Banner of Truth, 1976), 347-48: "Whoever puts away true and real wine, or fermented grape juice, on moral grounds, from the Lord's Supper sets himself up as more moral than the Son of God who reigns over his conscience, and than the Savior of souls who redeemed him."

identified these goods with gods. Dagon, the grain god of the Philistines, is mentioned in 1 Samuel 5:2-7. Tirosh was a Canaanite god of revelry and fertility—not the sort of imagery associated with unfermented grape juice.[2]

Nor is this claim supported in the New Testament. Recall Jesus' parable about new wine in old wineskins (Mt. 9:17; Mk. 2:22; Lk. 5:37-38): A beverage that bursts old and brittle wineskins suggests fermentation. In Acts 2:13 some ridiculed the apostles after hearing them speak in numerous languages, saying, "They are filled with new wine"! Clearly, the mockers weren't talking about grape juice; they associated new wine with its intoxicating effect.

Third and most important, opponents reject fermented wine on moral grounds. In various places, wine is mentioned in a negative light. After the flood, the morally upright Noah planted a vineyard, got drunk, and laid uncovered (Gen. 9:20-21). Elsewhere, Solomon was blunt in his assessment: "Wine is a mocker, strong drink a brawler, and whoever is led astray by it is not wise" (Prov. 20:1). Opponents of wine use these and other texts to promote total abstinence. This is why they argue for unfermented grape juice at the Cana wedding. Surely God in the flesh wouldn't promote drunkenness! Neither would he use fermented beverage in the sacrament.

Their point is well taken about the *misuse* of wine. Nevertheless, Scripture only condemns the use of wine that leads to drunkenness (Gen. 9:20-21: Prov. 23:21; Lk. 21:34; Rom. 13:13; Gal. 5:21; Eph. 5:18). These texts

---

[2] Victor Hamilton, *The Book of Genesis: Chapters 18-50*, 221.

suggest that drunkenness was a common sin in the ancient world. Even in such a culture, wine was commended for gladdening the heart and soothing the stomach. Since it was used in the old covenant sacrifices and Passover ritual, there's every reason to believe it was utilized in the Last Supper. The abuse of something should not disqualify its moderate use.

The Concession of Unfermented Grape Juice

The norm of the first century church should be the norm of the twenty-first century church: Fermented wine should be used in the Lord's Supper. Yet the modern world offers some challenges. To start, there are legal obstacles: Churches that rent may find landlords who are hostile to their practice. Some organizations, including churches, have restrictive language in their leases. Once signed, the lease must be honored. Additionally, some states prohibit the consumption of alcohol in public buildings.[3] In this situation, we're called to obey the civil magistrate (Rom. 13:1-7), even if it means using unfermented wine. Until a religious exception is granted, we are bound to follow the laws of the land.

This doesn't mean absolute submission in every circumstance. It would be different if civil law prohibited the preaching of the word, because there's no alternative. Not so the cup of the sacrament; while Scripture indicates the use of fermented wine, grape juice is at least a form of the fruit of the vine. Therefore, churches can afford to make concessions if necessary.

---

[3] This was the case in Independence, IA when my previous congregation rented the local civic center for worship.

There are also legitimate medical exceptions. People with particular health conditions or who take certain types of medication need to avoid alcohol. If churches are willing to make concessions for food allergies, they should do the same for beverages. Others struggle with addiction, still others bound by conscience. One could argue that the exclusive use of wine could be a stumbling block for an alcoholic or a barrier for a teetotaler (Rom. 14:1-6). If concessions can be made for medical conditions, then why not for other concerns? In situations like these, a mixed tray of wine and grape juice enables Christians on both sides to partake in unity. Since the Lord's Supper is the sacrament of the unity of the body, we should extend charity as far as we can when celebrating it.[4]

Even so, the exception should not become the rule; grape juice concessions should never supplant the biblical norm. To do so would violate liberty of conscience, denying Christians the opportunity to follow Christ's instructions. This also applies to legal situations that require the exception. Venues that forbid wine can never be considered permanent locations. They are stop-gap by nature, temporary landing spots until a better option comes along. The best options allow us to follow everything that Christ commanded (Mt.28:20).

---

[4] I'm indebted to David VanDrunen for this insight.

Chapter Seven

Ordained Waiters

Not every supper is the same. There's a considerable difference between a fast food eatery and a five-star restaurant. Fast food is quick and casual. You're there for the price, not necessarily the atmosphere, and service happens at the counter.

Five-star restaurants are different. These places are formal and deliberate. Since you're paying top dollar, you expect a pleasant atmosphere and attentive table service. Qualified waiters not only bring your meal and beverage, but know enough about the menu to advise and make recommendations. They're well-informed about the aging of beef and the best vintage of wine.

God offers us something better than a five-star restaurant: He invites us to His Supper. What can compare with the sacramental union of bread and wine with the body and blood of Christ? Even the finest cuisine pales in comparison. Such a meal requires a server who's not only knowledgeable about his fare, but ordained to the task.

This chapter focuses on the "ordained waiters" who serve the Lord's Supper—and makes the case from Scripture that this is a role for the pastor alone.

Biblical Support

The first ordained waiters were Old Testament priests. During the time of the patriarchs, Melchizedek, priest of God Most High, blessed Abraham verbally and by serving him bread and wine (Gen. 14:18). After the covenant at Sinai, the Levitical priests served the people of Israel in various ways. First, they fed them the word of God through public teaching (Deut. 31:9-11; Neh. 8:1-3; Mal. 2:7-9). Second, they administered a "sacramental" system of sacrifices (LEv. 6:8-38; cf. Heb. 5:1; 7:27; 9:26-28).[1] Third, they blessed the people by placing God's very name on them as a sign of ownership (Lev. 9:22, Num. 6:22-27).

Yet the Levitical priesthood wasn't an end in itself. It pointed to a Greater Priest who fulfilled their responsibilities. He not only taught the word, but has always been the eternal Word (Jn. 1:1; 14). In place of animal sacrifices to cover sin, He offered up Himself as the ultimate sacrifice (Heb. 2:17; 3:1; 8:1). And having completed His work on earth, He blessed His people (Lk. 24:50). Jesus Christ remains the Great High Priest who intercedes for His people (Heb. 7:25).

But if Jesus is presently sitting at the right hand of His Father, then who's presently serving here on earth? Since the priesthood is no longer tied to a tribe, some believe it's expanded to all Christians. All believers have become a "chosen race and holy nation" (Ex. 19:6; 1 Pet. 2:9-10) called to offer themselves as "living sacrifices" (Rom. 12:2; 1 Pet. 2:9). This is *the priesthood of all believers*, the service of every Christian.

---

[1] In particular, the peace offerings were shared among God, the priest, and the offeror (Lev. 7:19-21, 23-24).

But God hasn't given all the responsibilities of the priesthood to every Christian. Not everyone is called to preach the word, administer the sacraments, or pronounce the blessing. The first inheritors of these ministries were the apostles. Both priests and apostles were called to their office (Heb. 5:4; Acts 1:2; 1 Cor. 15:8-10) and given a ministry of word, sacrament, and blessing (Mt.10:1-8, 28:19, Jn. 4:1-2; 2 Cor. 13:14). The Apostle Paul also described his work in priestly categories. In Romans, he referred to his teaching ministry as "the priestly service of the gospel of God" for the purpose of making acceptable "the offering of the Gentiles, sanctified by the Holy Spirit" (Rom 15:15-16). In the Pastoral Epistles, he portrayed himself as a "drink offering poured on the altar" (2 Tim 4:6; cf. Ex. 29:40; Num. 18:7). He viewed his impending death in God's service as a "libation offered to God."[2] Even though the Levitical priesthood was fulfilled in Christ, Paul clearly identified himself as a spiritual successor.

The office of apostle was not given for all times and places. These men were part of the foundation of the church (Eph. 2:20) and Paul was the last of them (1 Cor. 15:8). They were succeeded by *presbyters*—also called overseers (Acts 20:28), evangelists (2 Tim. 4:5), teachers (1 Cor. 12:28), and pastors (1 Pet. 5:20). The word "presbyter" even encompasses two offices: (1) those who rule without teaching and (2) those who preach and teach (1 Tim. 5:17). Since this chapter is interested in the latter, we'll refer to them by the more common title: *Pastors*.

---

2 J.N.D. Kelly, *The Pastoral Epistles* (repr.; London: A & C Black, 1998), 208.

Like the priests and apostles before them, pastors feed their flocks by preaching and teaching God's word (1 Tim. 4:13; 2 Tim. 4:2), administering the sacraments (Acts 20:7; 1 Cor. 11:20), and pronouncing the blessing (Heb. 13:20-21). Paul spoke of both himself and his associates as "servants of Christ and stewards of the mysteries of God" (1 Cor. 4:1). The phrase "servants of Christ" describes religious functionaries instead of menial workers.[3] We know Paul functioned as an apostle, but what about his associates? Most likely they were pastors.

Paul and his associates were also called "stewards of the mysteries of God." In the ancient world, stewards watched over the possessions of others.[4] So what mysteries were being entrusted to them? In order to answer this question, we need to understand the nature of Biblical mysteries. Rather than being puzzles to be solved, these mysteries have already been revealed. Paul identified the gospel and the preaching of Christ as a mystery made known (Rom. 16:25; Eph. 6:9; Col. 4:3). To the Colossian church, he described his ministry as "the stewardship from God" concerning "the mystery hidden for ages and generations but now revealed to his saints ... which is Christ in you" (Col. 1:25-27). Thus, the mysteries of God involve the

---

3 Elsewhere *huperetes* refers to an officer assisting the priests (Lk. 4:20; Mk. 14:54; Jn. 7:32), a helper of apostles (Acts 13:5), and a minister of the word (Lk. 1:2).

4 David W. Gill, "1 Corinthians" in *Zondervan Illustrated Bible Backgrounds Commentary* (vol. 3; Clinton E. Arnold, gen. ed.; Grand Rapids: Zondervan, 2002), 123: "The word "entrusted" (*oikonomos*) was commonly used in the Hellenistic period of the person in charge of an estate belonging to an absentee landlord."

revelation of the gospel entrusted to the apostles and their successors.[5]

Yet notice the mysteries in 1 Corinthians 4 are plural. While there is only one gospel, it can be expressed in different forms. Gospel preaching involves audible words, while gospel sacraments express visible words. Jesus' words of institution are a case in point. "This cup that is poured out for you is the new covenant in my blood" (Lk. 22:20). The sensory wine is a visible sign connected to Christ's word; thus, its celebration imparts the mystery to God's people.

Today, pastors are the stewards of these mysteries. They are called to nourish the flock (Jn. 21:15; 1 Tim. 4:6), something achieved through word and sacrament. Consequently, pastors who continue these ministries of Old Testament priests and New Testament apostles should be the ones who administer the sacraments.

Practical Implications

The requirement of having pastors administer the sacrament leads to a number of implications. First and most obvious, it rules out the practice of self-administration. God's people who are unable to attend church due to health concerns would require a pastoral visit to receive the sacrament. A case can also be made that a representative number of the congregation should accompany the pastor, since the sacrament is intended to be a corporate feeding of the body of Christ (1 Cor. 10:17). Whatever the circumstance, Christians should not serve themselves.

---

[5] Gordon Fee, *The First Epistle to the Corinthians* (NICNT; Grand Rapids: Eerdmans, 1987), 160.

Second, it rules out other officiants. While it's true that the Lord's Supper is under the oversight of both pastors and elders, only the former can preside. Elders may assist in the distribution of the sacrament to facilitate orderly worship as long as a pastor is officiating. The reason has to do with the functional distinction between these two offices. Unlike pastors who succeed the priests and apostles in the ministry of word and sacrament, ruling elders follow the Old Testament elders of the people (Ex. 24:9; 2 Sam. 5:3; 1 Kgs. 8:1). These rulers exercised authority over Israel (Deut. 19:12; Josh. 20:4; Lk. 20:1), but their authority didn't carry over to the means of grace. This means that churches with vacant pulpits may not celebrate the sacrament unless guest pastors can fill the gap.

Finally, this serves as a corrective against the democratizing tendency in the modern church. Some Christians reject the distinction between clergy and laity out of a desire to promote equality. If we hold to the priesthood of all believers, then why would we need specialized "priests"? Why should only a few be able to preach, administer the sacraments, and pronounce blessings?

The answer is that God never intended the priesthood of all believers to displace the ordained servants of His Church. Paul made this point in 1 Corinthians 12. The body of Christ includes many members (v. 14), but not all of them have the same gifts and calling. Some were more prominent like the apostles and prophets (v. 28) while others less noticeable were just as indispensable (v. 22). The body of Christ today includes both teachers and helpers (v. 28) along with many other gifts. As the successors of priests and apostles, pastors have been given different gifts than other members in the church.

Unlike other members, they are set apart through ordination (laying on of hands) by the church (1 Tim. 4:14). Blurring the distinction between clergy and laity denies both the goodness of diverse gifts and the unique calling that God gives to pastors. Thus, linking the sacrament to these ordained waiters is a way of preserving this ancient distinction.

Unlike our common dining experiences that vary in atmosphere, pace, and price, the Lord's Supper offers an ecclesiastical atmosphere, a liturgical pace, and the priceless body and blood of Christ. For such a profound dining experience, God provides the servers. He ordains pastors to be the ordinary and perpetual waiters. Due to their gifts and calling, they continue as the exclusive servers of the sacrament.

Chapter Eight

Present and Future Feasting

The Lord's Supper is the sacred occasion for eating and drinking with God. The sacrament is food and drink for our souls, real communion with our risen Savior. Yet even though Jesus is present in the sacrament, he's invisible to our senses. Right now, we can't see, hear, smell or touch him, though one day we will. We already experience the real presence of our Savior, but one day we'll experience Him fully.

This chapter addresses the "already and not-yet" aspect of the Lord's Supper as we consider our present and future feasting. After defining this principle, we'll examine the words of our Lord in the Last Supper. In doing so, we'll consider how our present feasting involves Christ's abstinence while our future feasting entails a reunion with Christ's physical presence.

The "Already and Not Yet" Principle

The Bible teaches a present ("already") and future ("not yet") sense of our relationship with God.

[1]Currently, we're experiencing an "already" sense of communion with Christ. Jesus promised to be present through the bread and wine, and we receive this blessing by faith. Yet faith is different from sight; it is "the substance of things hoped for, the evidence of things not seen" (Heb. 11:1 KJV). One day faith will be superseded by sight, as we have sensory communion with our Savior. That's the "not yet" sense.

Present Feasting and Christ's Earthly Abstinence

Jesus spoke about the already and not yet principle in the Last Supper accounts. In Matthew and Mark, it occurs at the end of the text and only mentions the wine (Mt.26:29; Mk. 14:25). Luke, however, included it in the middle of his account and mentioned both food and wine (Lk. 22:15-18). For this reason, we'll consider Luke's account in detail. The evangelist wrote:

> And he said to them, "I have earnestly desired to eat this Passover with you before I suffer. For I tell you I will not eat it until it is fulfilled in the kingdom of God." And he took a cup, and when he had given thanks he said, "Take this, and divide it among yourselves. For I tell you that from now on I will not drink of the fruit of the vine until the kingdom of God comes."

Jesus' message involved both a present, earthly abstinence and a future, physical feasting. First, Jesus spoke about abstaining from food and wine. Why? Because His death on the cross was imminent. This Last Supper was His last Passover on earth. It was the

---

[1] Concerning the relationship of this principle to the kingdom of God, see my *Entering God's Rest: The Sabbath from Genesis to Revelation and What it Means for You* (Lancaster: Alliance of Confessing Evangelicals, 2018), 70f.

last old covenant meal He shared with his disciples. But the term "Last Supper" applies to the master, not to the disciples. The latter, as pilgrims along the way, would perpetuate the remembrance of this Last Passover in the form of the Lord's Supper. For the Last Supper ratified the new covenant while the Lord's Supper renews it going forward.

Christ's present earthly abstinence coincides with the already sense of the sacrament. His physical abstinence results from spatial and temporal separation. As we learned in chapter 2, Jesus' human nature is fixed in a particular space. He's in heaven while we're on earth. Thus, he can't physically partake of the new covenant meal with his people. Moreover, Christ's human nature is separated by time. He walked the earth in the first century while we do the same in the twenty-first century. Nevertheless, He's really present in the sacrament. We experience Him through the power of the Holy Spirit who transcends space and time. And we receive the blessings of this experience by faith. This is our present feasting.

Future Feasting in Physical Presence

Yet Christ's earthly abstinence won't last forever. He promised to eat and drink in the coming of the kingdom of God. This messianic banquet had its roots in the Old Testament where the prophet Isaiah foreshadowed "a feast of rich food, a feast of well-aged wine" for all people on the "mountain of the Lord" (Isa. 25:6). This mountaintop banquet would also be accompanied by God "swallowing up death forever" and "wiping away tears from all faces," (v. 8; cf. Rev. 21:4). These statements will find their fulfillment in our glorified state when Christ returns to make all things new (Rev. 21:1, 5a).

Like their presence in the Last Supper, the elements of food and wine are central images of this end-time feast. In other parts of his gospel, Luke made reference to Christ's statements concerning this event. He spoke of patriarchs, prophets, and people from every direction (i.e., Gentiles) reclining at table in the kingdom of God (13:28-29). While attending an earthly banquet, Jesus spoke about the "resurrection of the just" and one of the others spoke up and exclaimed, "Blessed is everyone who will eat bread in the kingdom of God" (14:14-15)![2]

The foreshadowing of the banquet in Isaiah and Luke finds fulfillment in Rev 19:7-9 in which the future feast is described in terms of a wedding:

> Let us rejoice and exult and give him the glory, for the marriage of the Lamb has come, and his Bride has made herself ready; it was granted her to clothe herself with fine linen, bright and pure for the fine linen is the righteous deeds of the saints. And the angel said to me, 'Write this: Blessed are those who are invited to the marriage supper of the Lamb.'

Here, the culmination of God's redemptive plan is described as a wedding feast. The corporate church is represented as the bride about to wed the Lamb in vv. 7-8 while individual Christians are portrayed as guests

---

[2] Christians will begin to experience this in the intermediate state. At death, our souls will separate from our bodies. The former transition to heaven and experience the risen Christ, while the latter remain on earth. Yet this is a temporary state since the inner man longs for the outer man. In Revelation 6:9-11, disembodied souls crying out for vengeance reveals a lack of resolution that can only come with the glorified state.

at the wedding feast in v. 9. Jesus who abstained from the earthly feast by ascending into heaven, now partakes with his bride-people in their state of glory.

Yet our future feasting isn't merely an intellectual curiosity; it reinforces our hope. Every time we celebrate the Sacrament of the Lord's Supper, we are reminded of this future certainty. Eating and drinking in the earthly sacrament assures us that we will partake of future and face-to-face glory with our Savior. As Christians, this is our blessed hope.

Appendix I

Supper, or Sacrifice?

We've already examined the view of transubstantiation. However, we ought to address another Roman Catholic (and Eastern Orthodox) teaching: The Eucharistic sacrifice, a concept that has provoked much hostility from Protestants.[1] In this view, the sacrament "re-presents (makes present) the sacrifice of the cross."[2]

---

[1] For example, WCF 29.2 states: "In this sacrament, Christ is not offered up to His Father; nor any real sacrifice made at all for remission of sins of the quick or dead; but only a commemoration of that one offering up of Himself, by Himself, upon the cross, once for all; and a spiritual oblation of all possible praises unto God for the same; so that the Popish sacrifice of the mass (as they call it) is most abominably injurious to Christ's one, only sacrifice, the alone propitiation for all the sins of His elect. See *Westminster Confession of Faith* (repr.; Glasgow, Free Presbyterian Publications, 2001), 116.

[2] *Catholic Catechism*, 1366, 380. Cf. Ware, *Orthodox Church*, 287: "The Eucharist is not a bare commemoration nor an imaginary representation of Christ's sacrifice, but the true sacrifice itself; yet on the other hand it is not a new sacrifice, nor a repetition of the sacrifice on Calvary, since the Lamb was sacrificed 'once only, for all time'. The events of Christ's sacrifice—the Incarnation, the Last Supper, the Crucifixion, the Resurrection, the Ascension—are not repeated in the Eucharist, but they are *made present*. During the Liturgy, through its divine power, we are projected to the point where eternity cuts across time, and at this point we become true *contemporaries* with the events which we commemorate."

For the sake of charitable dialogue, this appendix will consider the arguments and counter-arguments, while emphasizing the sacrament as a meal over a sacrifice.

First, Roman Catholics and Eastern Orthodox appeal to early church interpretations of Scripture. Many of the fathers viewed Malachi 1:10-11 as a foreshadowing of this sacramental sacrifice:

> For from the rising of the sun to its setting my name will be great among the nations, and in every place incense will be offered to my name, and a pure offering.[3]

Second, these traditions point to the Last Supper accounts in which Jesus instructed his disciples, "Do this in *remembrance* of me." The Greek word translated as "remembrance" is found in passages in the Greek Old Testament (LXX) describing sacrifices offered as acts of remembrance (Lev. 24:7; Num. 10:10; Ps. 38:1).[4] Moreover, the Last Supper accounts of Matthew and Mark included explicit words concerning the cup: "For this is my *blood* of the covenant, which is *poured out* for many for the forgiveness of sins." The notion of His blood being "poured out" recalls both the ratification ceremony for the Sinaitic covenant (Exod. 24:8) and the ongoing sacrifices of that covenant (Lev. 4:7).

Third, Paul wrote in 1 Corinthians chapter 10 about the Israelites "who eat the sacrifices" as those who

---

[3] See: Feingold, *Eucharist*, 130.

[4] J.N.D. Kelly, *Early Christian Doctrines* (rev. ed., San Francisco: Harper Collins, 1978), 196: "It was natural for early Christians to think of the eucharist as a sacrifice. The fulfillment of prophecy demanded a solemn Christian offering, and the rite itself was wrapped in the sacrificial atmosphere with which our Lord invested the Last Supper."

participate at the altar" (v. 18). Applying that to his New Testament readers, he contrasted participation in two different places: The "table of the Lord" against the "table of demons" (v.21). Despite the change in language from "altar" to "table", the context of sacrifice is still in view.[5] Paul wrote that "pagans sacrifice to demons and not to God" and warned God's people not to be "participants with demons" (v. 20). Instead, he urged them to be participants with God. And the means of participating would come through the sacrament: "The cup of blessing that we bless, is it not a participation in the blood of Christ? The bread that we break, is it not a participation in the body of Christ?" (v. 16) For these reasons, Roman Catholics and Eastern Orthodox argue that Lord's table is in fact His altar in which we participate.

These arguments deserve a fair response. One can acknowledge the connection between memorial and sacrifice and recognize that there is sacrificial language in the Last Supper accounts. But instead of a Eucharistic sacrifice, this language can just as easily be understood as type and fulfillment. Jesus's sacrifice fulfilled all the old covenant sacrifices which were done in remembrance of God's gracious actions.

This also affects the interpretation of Malachi 1:11. The context of vv. 10-14 involved blemished sacrifices that were profaning the Temple. Yet in the midst of corrupt worship, God promised to reform temple worship in

---

[5] The Greek word for "table" is sometimes used as a synonym for "altar" (Mal. 1:7, 12; Ezek 41:22). Malachi 1:7 even makes the connection explicit: "By offering polluted food upon my altar. But you say, 'How have we polluted you?' By saying that the Lord's table may be despised."

the future. He promised, "in every place incense will be offered to my name, and a pure offering." Since Malachi is the last Old Testament book, one would need to look to the New Testament to discover how His reform would take shape. It's found not a physical temple, but in the *fulfillment* of the temple. Jesus explained this to the woman at the well:

> The hour is coming when neither on this mountain nor in Jerusalem will you worship the Father. You worship what you do not know; We worship what we know, for salvation is from the Jews. But the hour is coming, and is now here, when the true worshipers will worship the Father in spirit and truth, for the Father is seeking such people to worship him (Jn. 4:21-23).

Christ was speaking about the end of the earthly temple because He provided a new and better temple: His very person! Jesus is the true Temple because He is both the ultimate high priest and the perfect sacrifice offered up "once for all", securing perfect redemption (Heb. 7:27; 9:12). A redemption that's already perfect means it doesn't need to be re-presented.[6] The very idea of an ongoing Eucharistic sacrifice is inconsistent with His once for all accomplishment.

The sacrifices that we're called to offer are *ourselves*. The Apostle Paul wrote, "I appeal to you therefore, brothers to present your bodies as a living sacrifice, holy and acceptable to God, which is your spiritual worship" (Rom. 12:1). The Apostle Peter reminded his audience, "you yourselves like living stones are being built up as a spiritual house, to be a holy priesthood, to offer spiritual sacrifices acceptable to God through

---

[6] Bavinck, Reformed Dogmatics, 4:573-74.

Jesus Christ" (1 Pet. 2:5). Using sacrificial language, the writer of Hebrews made this even more explicit:

> We have an altar from which those who serve the tent have no right to eat. For the bodies of those animals whose blood is brought into the holy places by the high priest as a sacrifice for sin are burned outside the camp. So Jesus also suffered outside the gate in order to sanctify the people through his own blood. Therefore, let us go to him outside the camp and bear the reproach he endured. For here we have no lasting city, but we seek the city that is to come. Through him then let us continually offer up a sacrifice of praise to God, that is, the fruit of lips that acknowledge his name. Do not neglect to do good and to share what you have, for such sacrifices are pleasing to God. (Heb. 13:10-16, my emphasis)

Rather than a Eucharistic sacrifice, these passages teach us something different: They show us that God requires the totality of our being as a sacrifice of praise and thanksgiving. The acts of remembrance and participation in the Lord's Supper are a part of our everything.

Rather than a propitiatory sacrifice, the Lord's Supper is presented to us as a meal. Whatever we bring to the sacrament is nothing compared with what we receive. And that's because the sacrament is gospel, not law. The Lord's sacrifice was an historical act; its benefits are available through union with Christ. But the Lord's Supper is an ongoing meal, an opportunity for eating and drinking with God. And by doing so, it's a means for growing in grace.

Appendix II

Infant Communion?

In Chapter 3, we saw why preparation should be one of the family expectations required for participating in the Lord's Supper. This involves a certain level of maturity; the instructions of worthy partaking, self-examination, and discerning the body all assume the ability to do so (1 Cor. 11:27-29).

Yet not everyone agrees with this assumption. Some would say that very young children aren't in view in 1 Corinthians 11. In their view, Paul was addressing those capable of preparation rather than other household members, including infants. While the view of *paedocommunion* has recently grown in popularity, it's been the practice of eastern Christianity for centuries.[1] So we shouldn't dismiss this view simply because it hasn't been normative in the west. In light of this, we'll consider the claims for paedocommunion and the biblical response to such claims.

The Context of 1 Corinthians 11

There's no doubt that 1 Corinthians 11:27-29 is *the* crucial text. Yet paedocommunion supporters disagree

---

[1] Bavinck, Reformed Dogmatics, 4:581.

that Paul had everyone in view when he required self-examination. For support, they point to the context of vv. 17-22 which spoke of *adult* disunity. Paul's warning, they say, was intended for those mature enough to practice self-reflection, not for very young children.

This argument, however, fails to take into account the language of 'whoever' (v. 27), 'let a person' (v. 28), and 'anyone' (v. 29) that Paul used in connection with self-examination and discernment. These words suggest that the apostle was establishing a universal principle about participating in the sacrament. Elsewhere in his epistles, he wrote to all the members including children (Eph. 6:1-3; Col. 3:20). So, when Paul speaks about "whoever" and "anyone," we should understand this as including children unless otherwise indicated.

The Issue of Old Testament Continuity

Paedocommunion supporters also appeal to the Old Covenant to bolster their argument. God's covenant with Abraham involved believers and their children. Abraham believed before he was circumcised (Rom. 4:9-11), but his children were circumcised before they believed (Gen. 17:10-13). In the old covenant, very young children attended covenant gatherings (Deut. 29:10-13; 2 Chron. 20:13; Joel 2:16) and took part in the Passover ritual (Ex. 12:26). Paedocommunion advocates believe these texts should inform Lord's Supper participation. They assert that since infants were circumcised in old covenant and are baptized in the new, so young children who participated in the Passover should participate in the Lord's Supper.

There are two problems with this comparison. First it assumes that children of any age participated in the Passover. Exodus 12:26-27 mentions children who are capable of asking questions, not infants. Second, the comparison asserts that the Passover and the Lord's Supper have a one to one relationship. The Last Supper was indeed a Passover meal, but the Lord's Supper had other precursors in the Old Testament. For example, Jesus's statement of the cup being "a new covenant in my blood" doesn't recall the Passover but the ratification of the Mosaic Covenant at Sinai (Ex. 24:8). Its sequel—a communion meal on the mountain—didn't involve children, but the leaders of Israel (v. 9). Another precursor, the old covenant peace offerings, were a shared meal between the offeror, the priests, and God (Lev. 7:19-21, 28-34). No mention is made of other family members participating in these communion meals. It's true the manna in the wilderness that prefigured Christ as the bread of life was eaten by entire households (Ex. 16; Jn. 6:31-35). Nevertheless, this clear example must be counterbalanced by the other precursors when determining suitable participants in the Lord's Supper.

Other Old Testament texts echo the lack of clarity regarding child participation. Some passages mention families being present at the festivals (Deut. 16:11, 14), while others suggest mature males attending the feasts (Deut. 16:16). For example, Jesus attended the Passover festival in the Temple when he was 12 years old, on the cusp of maturity in Judaism (Lk. 2:41-42). On the whole the data is varied, making it difficult to come to a definitive conclusion.

This touches upon the ancient interpretative strategy known as the *analogy of faith*. Sound biblical interpretation involves the clear interpreting the obscure and the New Testament interpreting the Old. As we've seen, the Old Testament data is inconclusive about child participation. While other New Testament texts are silent on this matter, 1 Corinthians 11:27-29 is crystal clear about its mature expectations for participation. This means that the analogy of faith supports preparation instead of paedocommunion.

Argument from Baptismal Regeneration

A third argument for paedocommunion sees it as a consequence of regeneration. In the early centuries of Christianity, infants allegedly received the Lord's Supper after being baptized. And there's some logic to this practice. If baptism grants new life (Jn. 3:5; Titus 3:5) washes away sins, and bestows the gift of the Spirit (Acts 2:38), then why should the baptized be denied the means of growth (Jn. 6:53)? This logic assumes that baptism regenerates those who receive it, a disputed claim among Christians (compare Acts 2:38 and 22:16 with 8:16). But even if we conceded this claim, it doesn't follow that the Lord's Supper should be given to infants if other conditions must also be met. Western Christians define these conditions as partaking worthily, self-examination, and discerning the body.

The issue of paedocommunion isn't a trivial academic debate. Paul included strong language of judgment against those who disregarded his warnings about preparation (1 Cor. 11:30-31). While that particular judgment may not be normative for all times and places, such language shows the seriousness of participating in the Lord's Supper. Historical precedents cannot override the testimony of Scripture. For these reasons, twenty-first century Christians should avoid the practice of paedocommunion.

About the Author

Ken Golden is the organizing pastor at Sovereign Grace Orthodox Presbyterian Church in Davenport, Iowa. He is the author of Presbytopia: What It Means to by Presbyterian and Entering God's Rest.

About the Alliance

The Alliance of Confessing Evangelicals is a coalition of pastors, scholars, and churchmen who hold the historic creeds and confessions of the Reformed faith and who proclaim biblical doctrine in order to foster a Reformed awakening in today's Church.

600 Eden Road, Lancaster, PA 17601
AllianceNet.org • 215-546-3696

BROADCASTING

The Bible Study Hour *Preparing you to think and act biblically.* Clear biblical preaching that serves as both a model to pastors and a stabilizing source of biblical truth for lay people featuring James Boice. TheBibleStudyHour.org

Every Last Word *Teaching the whole Bible to change your whole life.* A rich diet of expository preaching to help people grow and apply God's Word to everyday life with pastor, author, Christian college president Philip Ryken. EveryLastWord.org

Mortification of Spin *A casual conversation about things that count.* Culturally relevant and often controversial topics taken on in funny, thoughtful, and unpredictable ways with Aimee Byrd, Todd Pruitt, and Carl Trueman. MortificationofSpin.org

Theology on the Go *A brief conversation about eternal truths.* Join Jonathan Master and James Dolezal as they discuss important topics in a thoughtful and accessible way showing how theology is relevant today. TheologyontheGo.org

Dr. Barnhouse & the Bible *Making God's Word Plain.* Scholarly exposition of God's Word that is concise and captivating, with one of the most widely acclaimed American preachers for half a century, Donald Barnhouse. DrBarnhouse.org

The Alliance of Confessing Evangelicals is a coalition of pastors, scholars, and churchmen who hold the historic creeds and confessions of the Reformed faith and who proclaim biblical doctrine in order to foster a Reformed awakening in today's Church.

ALLIANCE
OF CONFESSING EVANGELICALS

600 Eden Road, Lancaster, PA 17601
AllianceNet.org • 215-546-3696

PUBLISHING

*reformation*21   **reformation21** *A Reformed perspective on current issues, grounding readers in the Word of God as proclaimed through the centuries.* Providing an authoritative, Reformed perspective on historic matters and current issues to inform, inspire, and challenge Christians. reformation21.org

Meet the Puritans *Where the dead still speak.* Sharing the theology and piety of the Puritans to reconnect Reformed Christians with their heritage, introduce evangelical Christians to this heritage, and give the world the answers this heritage provides. MeetthePuritans.org

 Place for Truth *Exploring the depths of what we believe.* Thoughtful yet accessible biblical, systematic, and practical theology, as well as church history exploring the importance and relevancy of what we believe. PlaceforTruth.org

Daily Devotionals from James Boice and Matthew Henry sent daily to complement your time in the Word. ThinkandActBiblically.org and MatthewHenry.org

Reformed Resources *70 Years of Reformed Resources.* Thousands of audio on both CD and MP3, video, book, booklet, and e-book resources from trustworthy authors and Alliance speakers. ReformedResources.org

EVENTS

Philadelphia Conference on Reformed Theology and Regional Events *Sound doctrine, boldly preached.* The oldest, continual, national Reformed conference in North America, and regional events including theology and Bible conferences. ReformedEvents.org

Reformation Societies *Encouraging, Emboldening, and Equipping.* Encouraging, emboldening, and equipping pastors and church leaders for the work of biblical reformation in the church. ReformationSocieties.org